COOKSHELF

Mediterranean

Anne White

This is a Parragon Book
First published in 2001

Parragon
Queen Street House
4 Queen Street
Bath BA1 1HE, UK

ISBN: 0-75255-496-4
ISBN: 0-75255-497-2

Printed in China

ACKNOWLEDGEMENTS

Editorial Consultant: Felicity Jackson
Editor: Julia Canning
Photography: Colin Bowling, Paul Forrester and Stephen Brayne
Home Economists: David Morgan, Vicki Smallwood and Gina Steer

All props supplied by Barbara Stewart at Surfaces.

NOTE

This book uses metric and imperial measurements.
Follow the same units of measurement throughout; do not mix metric and imperial.
All spoon measurements are level: teaspoons are assumed to be 5 ml,
and tablespoons are assumed to be 15 ml. Unless otherwise stated,
milk is assumed to be full fat, eggs are medium
and pepper is freshly ground black pepper.

Recipes using uncooked eggs should be
avoided by infants, the elderly, pregnant women, convalescents,
and anyone suffering from an illness.

Contents

Introduction

Anyone who has spent even the briefest amount of time along the Mediterranean cannot have come away without a lasting recollection of the wonderful aromas and flavours of the region. 'Robust' and 'intense' are just two of the appropriate adjectives to describe the range of dishes you find from coastal Spain through France, Italy, Greece and Turkey and along North Africa.

Most of the region's best-known dishes are, in essence, simple fare produced for generations from plentiful home-grown or local ingredients. To capture the true sun-kissed flavours of the region, it is important to seek out the best-quality produce. All the recipes in this book are simple and easy to prepare, but because most are so simple, they rely on ripe, flavour-filled ingredients for their character.

OLIVE OIL

Olive oils vary in colour from almost emerald green to the palest yellow, with flavours that range from peppery and spicy to very mild. There are even olive oils with a hint of chocolate.

If you are used to cooking with other vegetable oils, such as sunflower or corn, olive oil can be an acquired taste, and the only way to find the oils you like the most is to taste many. Olive oils are available in different grades. Extra-virgin is produced from the first pressing, so it has the fullest flavour and, consequently, is the most expensive. Save this to use in salad dressings and with uncooked ingredients, where heat doesn't diminish the flavour. For cooking, choose an oil simply labelled as 'olive oil'.

Much is made of the healthy qualities of the Mediterranean diet, because olive oil contains so little saturated fat, the type of fat possibly linked to heart disease. But remember, it is still a fat, so it should be used sparingly, rather than with abandon.

TOMATOES

Sun-ripened, juicy tomatoes give flavour to both cooked and uncooked Mediterranean dishes. When you can only buy insipid hot-house tomatoes, a good-quality canned variety is a better option for cooked dishes. Italian plum tomatoes are a good choice, but the larger tomatoes and small cherry tomatoes are also ideal for many recipes. When you are buying tomatoes, look for smooth, undamaged skins and textures that feel just soft when you squeeze lightly. Try preserving tomatoes as Oven-dried Tomatoes (see page 174) to use in the colder months. When you have a large quantity of tomatoes lacking in flavour, use them for recipes such as Slow-cooked Tomato Sauce (see page 192) or Ratatouille (see page 134), both of which freeze well and have other ingredients that compensate for the weak tomato flavour.

GARLIC

Garlic is the all-important flavouring in many Mediterranean dishes, and it is also used both cooked and uncooked. Raw garlic can be too strong for some people, but when cooked slowly its flavour softens and whole cloves become meltingly soft and deliciously sweet.

Do not buy garlic bulbs that have sprouted because that is a sign that they are old and may taste bitter. The best garlic has compact cloves and tight-fitting skin. Do not store it in the refrigerator – it keeps best at room temperature in a dark location.

> *Roasted Garlic* Delicious smeared on grilled chicken pieces or steaks, or on toasted bread. Put a whole bulb of unpeeled garlic in a piece of foil, large enough to enclose it, and drizzle with olive oil. Roast in a preheated oven at 190°C/375°F/Gas Mark 5 for 40 minutes, or until the cloves are very soft when pierced with a knife. Squeeze the cloves out of their papery skins.

AUBERGINES

Elongated aubergines, with their deep-purple smooth skins, also symbolize Mediterranean cooking to many people – they are an essential ingredient to the French and Italians.

Many recipes specify sprinkling cut pieces of aubergine with salt and leave the pieces to stand for about 30 minutes before using. This simple technique draws out moisture to prevent the flesh becoming soggy and helps to eliminate bitterness, which is a characteristic of older aubergines. After they have drained, rinse them well to remove the excess salt. If the aubergine slices are going to be baked or fried, pat them dry with kitchen paper first.

At the height of summer, Mediterranean market stalls are piled high with miniature varieties of aubergines with pale purple or almost-white skins. These make attractive appetizers or garnishes. Only buy aubergines that feel smooth and firm. Size doesn't affect the flavour, but remember that the thicker an aubergine is, the more seeds it is likely to contain. Aubergines have a natural affinity with tomatoes, so you'll often find the two ingredients combined.

SEAFOOD

With the teeming waters of the Mediterranean, it is not surprising that fish and shellfish feature regularly in the local diets. Bouillabaisse, the classic French seafood stew, is an example of the wonderful use made of the daily catches. But the dish is expensive, so instead enjoy the flavour with the scaled-down version of Seafood Stew (see page 100), or Mediterranean Fish Soup (see page 98).

Whether you are buying fresh fish or shellfish, the golden rule is the same – only buy the freshest available and cook it on the same day. Fresh fish should have clear, shiny eyes and red gills. When you pick up a whole fish, it should be firm, not floppy. If it droops, it has been out of the water for more than a day and should be left on the fish counter.

Cut pieces of fish, such as swordfish or tuna steaks, should have a clear, clean-looking surface. White fish, such as a sea bass, should have a pearl-like colour.

Fish should not smell 'fishy'. Instead, it should have a fresh, almost sweet aroma, as if it has come out of the water only a few hours before.

Remember that shellfish, such as mussels, oysters and clams, should actually be alive when you buy them. You can tell they are fresh if their shells are closed. Prawns, on the other hand, are usually frozen before they are shipped.

As a general rule, the less time you cook seafood the better the flavour and texture will be.

FRESH HERBS

If you drive along the Mediterranean coast in summer, you will find the air is scented with rosemary, basil, coriander, dill, oregano, sage, flat-leaved parsley and thyme growing in profusion. Winter stews and casseroles use dried herbs, but only the freshest, fullest-flavoured herbs will do for the summer dishes and salads. The obvious solution if you plan to do a lot of Mediterranean cooking is to grow your own, so you always have a supply. Even a single pot of various herbs on your windowsill will make a difference to your cooking.

When you are buying fresh herbs, reject any that do not look fresh and vibrant; limp, dull-looking herbs without their full aroma will not add anything to your dish. Be sure to sniff the herbs before you buy, however, because greenhouse-grown ones can look fantastic but lack the essential flavour.

Basil Where would Italian cooks be without this fragrant herb? It has an affinity with tomatoes and is often included in pasta dishes and soups. It is difficult to preserve successfully, so if you have a glut, freeze large quantities of Pesto Sauce (see page 124) or Pistou sauce (see page 28). Do not freeze the leaves because they will turn black and lose their aroma. Instead, layer them with sea salt in a non-metallic, tightly covered container and leave for up to 3 months. They can then be added to cooked dishes.

Coriander Also popular in Asian cooking, this herb has a distinctive taste. It is used in many Turkish, Moroccan and Greek recipes. Be careful when buying it because it looks similar to flat-leaved parsley and often the only way to tell them apart is to taste a leaf.

Dill This feathery green herb with its distinctive flavour goes well with all seafood and tomato dishes, and is particularly used in Greek cooking.

Parsley Mediterranean cooks favour the flat-leaved variety of this all-purpose herb. Use in salads and as a garnish. Always use fresh or frozen, and avoid dried.

Marjoram The Greeks consider this the 'joy of the mountains' and it features in the islands' cuisines. It is good with pork and poultry dishes.

Oregano Also known as wild marjoram, this pungent herb should be used sparingly. It dries well, making a good addition to winter casseroles and pizzas. Try it with tomato, courgette and aubergine dishes.

Rosemary This strongly-flavoured shrub herb should be very young if used in uncooked dishes. It's a natural partner to lamb. Throw branches on barbecue coals to add an authentic aroma, or use twigs as skewers.

Sage Popular both fresh and dried in Italian dishes, sage has a pronounced flavour. Good for boiling with beans and for flavouring grilled poultry, the purple-leaved variety also makes an attractive garnish.

Thyme The small leaves are good for flavouring tomatoes, stews and grilled meats. Thyme also goes well with olives.

Herbes de Provence When you have an abundance of summer herbs, use them to make this classic French combination of herbs and spices. Dry equal amounts of fennel seeds, lavender flowers, marjoram, rosemary, sage, summer savory and thyme. Put them into an airtight container and store for up to 6 months.

Herbes de Provence is traditionally used to flavour cooked poultry, meat and vegetable dishes, especially during the winter. This combination of herbs is also good in cooked pasta sauces and pizza toppings.

Snacks
& Starters

One of the most enjoyable aspects of Mediterranean cuisines
is the emphasis on snacks and simple dishes that are served at
almost any time of the day. The Spanish, for example, are
renowned for their tapas, and the Greeks, Turks and
Moroccans enjoy nothing more than sitting down at a table
filled with a selection of appetizers, called meze.

The recipes in this chapter are easy to prepare and always
popular because they are so flavourful. They are also the type
of food to enjoy at relaxed, social occasions, and recipes such
as Hummus, Taramasalata, Tapenade, Aubergine Spread,
and Aioli, instantly capture the atmosphere of easy-going,
sunny Mediterranean meals.

When it's a hot day and you don't want to spend time in a
steaming kitchen, where better to look for inspiration than
the Mediterranean? For no-cook recipes, try the Gazpacho,
Garlic & Almond Soup, or Ceviche, along with any of the
mouthwatering dips listed above. And what can possibly beat
Parma Ham with melon and figs on a summer day? If you
want a sophisticated start for a meal, but again don't want to
cook, try Crab & Celeriac Remoulade. Serve it with a
chilled bottle of Provençal rosé and your dinner will be off to
a fantastic start.

Hummus

Makes about 700 g/1 lb 9 oz

INGREDIENTS

200 g/7 oz dried chickpeas
2 large garlic cloves
7 tbsp extra-virgin olive oil

2½ tbsp tahini
1 tbsp lemon juice, or to taste
salt and pepper

TO GARNISH
extra-virgin olive oil
paprika
fresh coriander

1 Place the chickpeas in a large bowl. Pour in at least twice the volume of cold water to beans and leave to stand for at least 12 hours until they double in size.

2 Drain the chickpeas. Put them in a large flameproof casserole or saucepan and add twice the volume of water to beans. Bring to the boil and boil hard for 10 minutes, skimming the surface.

3 Lower the heat and leave to simmer for 1 hour, or until the chickpeas are tender, skimming the surface if necessary. Meanwhile, cut the garlic cloves in half, remove the pale green or white cores and coarsely chop. Set aside.

4 Drain the chickpeas, reserving 4 tablespoons of the cooking liquid. Put the olive oil, garlic, tahini and lemon juice in a food processor and blend until a smooth paste forms.

5 Add the chickpeas and blend gently until they are finely ground but the hummus is still slightly textured. Add a little of the reserved cooking liquid if the mixture is too thick. Season with salt and pepper to taste.

6 Transfer to a bowl, cover with cling film and chill until ready to serve. To serve, drizzle with some olive oil, sprinkle a little paprika over the surface and garnish with fresh coriander.

Taramasalata with Pitta Wedges

Makes about 450 g / 1 lb

INGREDIENTS

225 g/8 oz smoked cod's roe
1 small onion, finely chopped
1 garlic clove
60 g/2¼ oz fresh white bread
    without crusts
4 tbsp lemon juice, plus extra to
    taste, if wished

finely grated rind of 1 lemon
150 ml/5 fl oz extra-virgin
    olive oil
6 tbsp hot water
salt and pepper
hollowed-out tomatoes, to serve

fresh flat-leaved parsley sprigs,
    to garnish

PITTA WEDGES
2 pitta breads
olive oil, for brushing

1 Remove the skin from the smoked cod's roe. Put the roe and onion in a food processor and process until well blended and smooth. Add the garlic and process again.

2 Break the bread into the food processor, then add 4 tablespoons of the lemon juice and the lemon rind. Process again until the bread is well incorporated.

3 With the motor running, gradually add the olive oil through the feed tube, as if making a mayonnaise. When all the oil is incorporated, add the hot water and process again. Add salt and pepper to taste, plus extra lemon juice if wished. Spoon into a bowl, cover with cling film and chill until ready to serve.

4 To make the pitta wedges, using a serrated knife, cut the pitta breads in half through the centre. Cut each half into 6–8 wedges, depending on the size. Place on a baking sheet and brush the inside surfaces of the wedges with olive oil.

5 Bake in a preheated oven at 180°C/350°F/Gas Mark 4 for 20 minutes. Leave to cool on wire racks.

6 Spoon the taramasalata into the tomato shells, garnish with parsley and serve with the pitta wedges for dipping.

Tzatziki

Makes about 750 g /1 lb 10 oz

INGREDIENTS

2 large cucumbers
600 ml/1 pint Greek Strained
  Yogurt (see page 182), or
  natural thick yogurt

3 garlic cloves, crushed
1 tbsp finely chopped fresh dill
1 tbsp extra-virgin olive oil
salt and pepper

TO SERVE
1 tbsp sesame seeds
cayenne pepper
fresh dill sprigs (optional)

1 Using the coarse side of a grater, grate the cucumbers into a bowl lined with an absorbent, perforated kitchen cloth. Pull up the corners of the cloth to make a tight bundle and squeeze very hard to extract all the moisture (see Cook's Tip).

2 Put the cucumbers in a bowl. Stir in the yogurt, garlic, dill, olive oil and salt and pepper to taste. Cover with cling film and chill for at least 3 hours for the flavours to blend.

3 When ready to serve, remove the dip from the refrigerator and stir. Taste the mixture and adjust the seasoning if necessary.

4 Put the sesame seeds in a small, ungreased frying pan and dry-fry them over a medium heat until they turn golden and start to give off their aroma. Immediately pour them out of the pan and on to the tzatziki – where they will sizzle.

5 Lightly dip the tip of a dry pastry brush into some cayenne pepper. Tap a light sprinkling of cayenne all over the tzatziki. Garnish with fresh dill, if wished, and serve.

COOK'S TIP

It is essential to squeeze all the moisture out of the cucumbers in Step 1, or the dip will be watery and separate.

COOK'S TIP

The ungarnished tzatziki will keep, covered, for up to 3 days in the refrigerator.

Aubergine Spread

Makes about 400 g / 14 oz

INGREDIENTS

2 large aubergines
1 tomato
1 garlic clove, chopped
4 tbsp extra-virgin olive oil
2 tbsp lemon juice

2 tbsp pine kernels, lightly
    toasted
2 spring onions, finely chopped
salt and pepper

TO GARNISH
ground cumin
2 tbsp finely chopped fresh
    flat-leaved parsley

1 Using a fork or metal skewer, pierce the aubergines all over. Place them on a baking sheet in a preheated oven at 230°C/450°F/Gas Mark 8 and roast for 20–25 minutes until they are very soft.

2 Use a folded tea towel to remove the aubergines from the baking sheet and set aside to cool.

3 Place the tomato in a heatproof bowl, pour boiling water over to cover and leave to stand for 30 seconds. Drain, then plunge into cold water to prevent it from cooking. Skin the tomato, then cut in half and scoop out the seeds with a teaspoon. Finely dice the flesh and set aside.

4 Cut the aubergines in half lengthways. Scoop out the flesh with a spoon and transfer to a food processor. Add the garlic, olive oil, lemon juice, pine kernels, and salt and pepper to taste. Process the mixture until smooth.

5 Spoon the mixture into a bowl and stir through the spring onions and diced tomato. Cover and chill for 30 minutes before serving.

6 Garnish the dip with a pinch of ground cumin and the finely chopped parsley, then serve.

VARIATION

Add 2–4 tablespoons of tahini, to taste, in Step 4.

Tapenade

Each makes about 300g / 10½oz

INGREDIENTS

BLACK OLIVE TAPENADE
250 g/9 oz black Niçoise olives
    in brine, rinsed and stoned
1 large garlic clove
2 tbsp walnut pieces
4 canned anchovy fillets, drained
about 125 ml/4 fl oz extra-virgin
    olive oil
lemon juice, to taste
pepper

GREEN OLIVE TAPENADE
250 g/9 oz green olives in brine,
    rinsed and stoned
4 canned anchovy fillets, rinsed
4 tbsp blanched almonds
1 tbsp bottled capers in brine or
    vinegar, rinsed
about 125 ml/4 fl oz extra-virgin
    olive oil
pepper

½–1 tbsp finely grated
    orange rind

CROUTES
thin slices of day-old
    baguette (optional)
olive oil (optional)
fresh flat-leaved parsley sprigs,
    finely chopped, to garnish

1 To make the black olive tapenade, put the olives, garlic, walnut pieces and anchovies in a food processor and process until blended.

2 With the motor running, slowly add the olive oil through the feed tube, as if making mayonnaise. Add lemon juice and pepper to taste. Transfer to a bowl, cover with cling film and chill until required.

3 To make the green olive tapenade, put the olives, anchovies, almonds and capers in a food processor and process until blended.

4 With the motor running, slowly add the olive oil through the feed tube, as if making mayonnaise. Add the orange rind and pepper to taste. Transfer to a bowl, cover with cling film and chill until required.

5 Serve the tapenade on croûtes. Toast the slices of bread on both sides until crisp. Brush one side of each slice with a little olive oil while it is still hot, so the oil is absorbed.

6 Spread the croûtes with the tapenade of your choice and garnish with a sprinkling of parsley.

Bagna Cauda

Serves 4–6

INGREDIENTS

50 g/1¾ oz canned anchovy
   fillets in oil
2 garlic cloves
5 tbsp olive oil

85 g/3 oz butter

TO SERVE
red and green peppers

courgettes
carrots
small broccoli florets

1 Begin by preparing the vegetables for dipping. Cut the peppers in half, remove the cores and seeds and slice into 5 mm/¼ inch strips. Cut the courgettes and carrots into 5 mm/¼ inch strips. Place in a plastic bag and chill until required.

2 Drain the anchovy fillets, reserving 5 tablespoons of the oil. Then chop the anchovies and garlic. Put the anchovy oil and olive oil in a saucepan with the butter over a high heat and stir until the butter melts.

3 Lower the heat to medium and add the garlic. Stir for 2 minutes, without letting it burn. Add the anchovies and allow them to simmer for about 10 minutes, stirring frequently, until they dissolve and turn the mixture into a thin paste.

4 Transfer the dip to a bagna cauda or fondue burner to keep it hot while you are eating. Serve with a platter of the prepared peppers, courgettes, carrots and broccoli for dipping.

VARIATION

This full-flavoured dip has a natural affinity with the sun-kissed vegetables from the Mediterranean, but you can serve it with any selection you like. Other suggestions include blanched white or green asparagus spears, blanched baby artichokes, blanched French beans and cauliflower florets.

Iced Gazpacho

Serves 4–6

INGREDIENTS

2 ripe red peppers
1 cucumber
400 g/14 oz large, juicy
    tomatoes, skinned, deseeded
    and coarsely chopped
4 tbsp olive oil
2 tbsp sherry vinegar
salt and pepper

GARLIC CROUTONS
2 tbsp olive oil
1 garlic clove, halved
2 slices bread, crusts
    removed and cut into
    5 mm/¼ inch dice
sea salt

TO GARNISH
diced green pepper
diced red pepper
finely diced deseeded cucumber
chopped spring onions
ice cubes

1 Cut the peppers in half and remove the cores and seeds, then coarsely chop. Peel the cucumber, cut it in half lengthways, then cut into quarters. Remove the seeds with a teaspoon, then coarsely chop the flesh.

2 Put the peppers, cucumber, tomatoes, olive oil and sherry vinegar in a food processor and process until smooth. Season with salt and pepper to taste. Transfer to a bowl, cover and chill for at least 4 hours.

3 Meanwhile, make the garlic croûtons. Heat the oil in a frying pan over a medium–high heat. Add the garlic and fry, stirring, for 2 minutes to flavour the oil.

4 Remove and discard the garlic. Add the diced bread and fry until golden on all sides. Drain well on crumpled kitchen paper and sprinkle with sea salt. Store in an airtight container if not using at once.

5 To serve, place each of the vegetable garnishes in bowls for guests to add to their soup. Taste the soup and adjust the seasoning if necessary. Put ice cubes into soup bowls and ladle the soup on top. Serve at once.

Chilled Garlic & Almond Soup

Serves 4–6

INGREDIENTS

400 g/14 oz day-old French bread, sliced	6 tbsp extra-virgin olive oil	TO GARNISH
4 large garlic cloves	225 g/8 oz ground almonds	seedless white grapes, chilled and sliced
3–4 tbsp sherry vinegar	sea salt and pepper	pepper
1 litre/1¾ pints water, chilled		extra-virgin olive oil

1 Tear the bread into small pieces and put in a bowl. Pour over enough cold water to cover and leave to soak for 10–15 minutes. Using your hands, squeeze the bread dry. Transfer the moist bread to a food processor.

2 Cut the garlic cloves in half lengthways and use the tip of the knife to remove the pale green or white cores. Add to the food processor with 3 tablespoons of sherry vinegar and 225 ml/8 fl oz of water, and process until blended. Add the oil and ground almonds and blend.

3 With the motor running, slowly pour in the remaining water until a smooth soup forms. Add extra sherry vinegar to taste and season with salt and other pepper. Transfer to a bowl, cover, and chill the soup for at least 4 hours.

4 To serve, adjust the seasoning. Ladle into bowls and float grapes on top. Garnish each with a sprinkling of pepper and a swirl of olive oil. Serve while still cold.

COOK'S TIP

Chilled grapes are the traditional accompaniment for this, but many other ingredients are suitable. Try the Garlic Croûtons and the diced vegetables suggested with the gazpacho recipe (see page 20). For garlic-lovers, fry thin slices of garlic in olive oil until golden brown, then sprinkle over to add a crunchy contrast to the soup. Or sprinkle lightly with paprika or very finely chopped fresh parsley just before serving.

Avgolemono

Serves 4–6

INGREDIENTS

1.2 litres/2 pints home-made
chicken stock
100 g/3½ oz dried orzo, or other
small pasta shapes

2 large eggs
4 tbsp lemon juice
salt and pepper

TO GARNISH
finely chopped fresh
flat-leaved parsley

1 Pour the stock into a
flameproof casserole or
heavy-based saucepan and
bring to the boil. Sprinkle
in the orzo, return to the
boil and cook for 8–10
minutes, or according to
packet instructions, until the
pasta is tender.

2 Whisk the eggs in a bowl,
for at least 30 seconds.
Add the lemon juice and
continue whisking for a
further 30 seconds.

3 Reduce the heat under
the pan of stock and
orzo until the stock is no
longer boiling.

4 Very slowly add 4–5
tablespoons of the hot
(not boiling) stock to the
lemon and egg mixture,
whisking constantly. Slowly
add another 225 ml/8 fl oz of
the stock, whisking to
prevent the eggs curdling.

5 Slowly pour the lemon
and egg mixture into the
pan, whisking until the soup
thickens slightly. Do not
allow it to boil. Season with
salt and pepper.

6 Spoon the soup into
warmed soup bowls and
sprinkle with chopped flat-
leaved parsley. Serve at once.

VARIATION

*To make a more
substantial soup, add
300 g/10½ oz finely
chopped, cooked,
skinless chicken meat.
This version uses orzo,
a small pasta shape that
looks like barley grains,
but you can substitute
long-grain rice.*

Roasted Pepper &
Tomato Soup with Dill

Serves 6–8

INGREDIENTS

1 kg/2 lb 4 oz juicy plum
   tomatoes, halved
2 large red peppers, cored,
   deseeded and halved
1 onion, quartered

3 sprigs fresh dill, tied together,
   plus a little extra to garnish
1 thin piece of orange rind
juice of 1 orange
600 ml/1 pint vegetable stock

salt and pepper
1–1½ tbsp red wine vinegar
Mediterranean Bread (see page
   198), to serve

1 Place the tomatoes and peppers on a baking sheet, cut-sides up to catch the juices. Add the onion quarters. Place in a preheated oven at 230°C/450°F/Gas Mark 8 and roast for 20–25 minutes until the vegetables just start to char on the edges.

2 As the vegetables become charred, transfer them to a large flameproof casserole or stockpot. Add the dill, orange rind and juice, stock and salt and

pepper to taste. Bring to the boil.

3 Lower the heat, partially cover and simmer for 25 minutes. Remove the bundle of dill and transfer the rest of the ingredients to a food mill (see Cook's Tip) and purée. Alternatively, process in a food processor and work through a fine sieve.

4 Return the soup to the rinsed casserole or stockpot and reheat. Stir in the vinegar and adjust the

seasoning with salt and pepper, if necessary. Ladle into bowls and garnish with extra dill. Serve hot, with slices of Mediterranean Bread (see page 198).

COOK'S TIP

A food mill, or mouli-légume as it is called in France, is ideal for puréeing vegetable soups and sauces because it removes the skin and seeds in the process.

Pistou

Serves 6–8

INGREDIENTS

2 young carrots	2.5 litres/4½ pints vegetable	PISTOU SAUCE
2 potatoes	stock or water	75 g/2¾ oz fresh basil leaves
200 g/7 oz fresh peas in	1 bouquet garni of 2 sprigs fresh	1 garlic clove
their shells	parsley and 1 bay leaf tied in	5 tbsp fruity extra-virgin olive oil
200 g/7 oz thin French beans	a 7.5 cm/3 inch piece of celery	salt and pepper
150 g/5½ oz young courgettes	1 large tomato, skinned, deseeded	
2 tbsp olive oil	and chopped or diced	
1 garlic clove, crushed	85 g/3 oz small dried soup pasta	
1 large onion, finely chopped	pared Parmesan cheese, to serve	

1 To make the pistou sauce, put the basil leaves, garlic and olive oil in a food processor and process until well blended. Season with salt and pepper to taste. Transfer to a bowl, cover and chill until required.

2 Peel the carrots and cut them in half lengthways, then slice. Peel the potatoes and cut into quarters lengthways, then slice. Set aside.

3 Shell the peas. Top and tail the beans and cut them into 2.5 cm/1 inch pieces. Cut the courgettes in half lengthways, then slice.

4 Heat the oil in a large saucepan or flameproof casserole. Add the garlic and fry for 2 minutes, stirring. Add the onion and continue frying for 2 minutes until soft. Add the carrots and potatoes and stir for about 30 seconds.

5 Pour in the stock and bring to the boil. Lower the heat, partially cover and simmer for 8 minutes, until the vegetables are starting to become tender.

6 Stir in the peas, beans, courgettes, bouquet garni, tomato and pasta. Season and cook for 4 minutes, or until the vegetables and pasta are tender. Stir in the pistou sauce and serve with Parmesan.

Parma Ham with Fruit

Serves 4

INGREDIENTS

1 cantaloupe or Charentais
melon
4 ripe fresh figs (optional)

12 wafer-thin slices Parma ham
olive oil, to drizzle
pepper

fresh parsley sprigs, to garnish

1 Cut the melon in half
lengthways. Using a
spoon, scoop out the seeds
and discard them. Cut each
half into 8 thin wedges.
Using a paring knife, cut the
rind off each slice.

2 Cut the stems off the
figs, if using, but do not
peel them. Stand the figs
upright with the pointed
end upwards. Cut each into
quarters without cutting all
the way through. Open them
out into attractive 'flowers'.

3 Arrange 3–4 slices of
Parma ham on individual
serving plates and top with
the melon slices and fig
'flowers', if using.
Alternatively, arrange the
melon slices on the
plates and completely cover
with the ham; add the figs,
if using.

4 Drizzle with olive oil,
then grind a little pepper
over the top. Garnish with
parsley and serve at once.

COOK'S TIP

*For an attractive
presentation, you can
also prepare all the
ingredients on one large
serving platter and let
guests help themselves.*

VARIATION

*For a Spanish flavour,
replace the Parma ham
with Serrano ham, which
also has a slightly salty
flavour but is rarely cut
as finely.*

Chorizo & Chickpea Tapas

Serves 4

INGREDIENTS

7 tbsp olive oil
about 2 tbsp sherry vinegar
250 g/9 oz fresh chorizo sausage,
   in one piece

1 small Spanish onion,
   chopped finely
400 g/14 oz canned chickpeas
salt and pepper

finely chopped fresh oregano or
   flat-leaved parsley, to garnish
chunks of fresh bread, to serve

1 Place 6 tablespoons of the olive oil and 2 tablespoons of the sherry vinegar in a bowl and whisk together. Taste and add a little more sherry vinegar, if desired. Season with salt and pepper and set aside.

2 Using a small, sharp knife, remove the casing from the chorizo sausage. Cut the sausage meat into 5 mm/¼ inch thick slices, then cut each slice into half-moon shapes.

3 Heat the remaining olive oil in a small frying pan over a medium-high heat. Add the onion and fry for 2–3 minutes, stirring. Add the chorizo sausage and cook for 3 minutes, or until the sausage is cooked through.

4 Using a slotted spoon, remove the sausage and onion and drain on crumpled kitchen paper. Transfer to the bowl with the dressing while still hot and stir together.

5 Empty the chickpeas into a sieve and rinse well under running water; shake off the excess water. Add to the bowl with the other ingredients and stir together. Leave to cool.

6 Just before serving, adjust the seasoning, then spoon the salad into a serving bowl and sprinkle with chopped herbs. Serve with chunks of fresh bread.

Dolmas

Makes 25–30

225 g/8 oz package vine leaves
preserved in brine, about
40 in total
150 ml/5 fl oz olive oil
4 tbsp lemon juice
300 ml/10 fl oz water
lemon wedges, to serve

FILLING
125 g/4½ oz long-grain rice,
not basmati
350 ml/12 fl oz water
60 g/2¼ oz currants
60 g/2¼ oz pine kernels, chopped
2 spring onions, very finely
chopped

4 tbsp very finely chopped
fresh parsley
1 tbsp each of very finely
chopped fresh coriander
and dill
finely grated rind of ½ lemon
salt and pepper

1 Rinse the vine leaves and place them in a heatproof bowl. Pour over enough boiling water to cover and leave to soak for 5 minutes. Drain well.

2 Meanwhile, place the rice and water in a pan with a pinch of salt and bring to the boil. Lower the heat, cover, and simmer for 10–12 minutes, or until all the liquid is absorbed. Drain and set aside to cool.

3 Stir the currants, pine kernels, spring onions, herbs and lemon rind into the cooled rice. Season well with salt and pepper.

4 Line the bottom of a large frying pan with 3 or 4 of the thickest vine leaves, or any that are torn.

5 Put a vine leaf on the work surface, vein-side upwards, with the pointed end facing away from you. Put a small, compact roll of the stuffing at the base of the leaf. Fold up the bottom end of the leaf.

6 Fold in each side to overlap in the centre. Roll up the leaf around the filling. Squeeze lightly in your hand. Continue this process with the remaining vine leaves.

7 Place the leaf rolls in a single layer in the pan, seam-side down. Combine the olive oil, lemon juice and water and pour into the pan.

8 Fit a heatproof plate over the rolls and cover the pan. Simmer for 30 minutes. Remove from the heat and leave the stuffed vine leaves to cool in the liquid. Serve chilled with lemon wedges.

Grilled Sardines

Serves 4–6

INGREDIENTS

12 sardines	DRESSING	4 shallots, thinly sliced
olive oil	150 ml/5 fl oz extra-virgin	1 small fresh red chilli, deseeded
fresh flat-leaved parsley sprigs,	olive oil	and finely chopped
to garnish	finely grated rind of	1 large garlic clove, finely
lemon wedges, to serve	1 large lemon	chopped
	4 tbsp lemon juice, or to taste	salt and pepper

1 To make the dressing, place all the ingredients in a screw-top jar, season with salt and pepper, then shake until blended. Pour into a non-metallic baking dish that is large enough to hold the sardines in a single layer. Set aside.

2 To prepare the sardines, chop off the heads and make a slit all along the length of each belly. Pull out the insides, rinse the fish inside and out with cold water and pat dry with kitchen paper.

3 Line the grill pan with foil, shiny side up. Brush the foil with a little olive oil to prevent the sardines sticking. Arrange the sardines on the foil in a single layer and brush with a little of the dressing. Cook under a preheated grill for about 90 seconds.

4 Turn the fish over, brush with a little more dressing and continue grilling for 90 seconds, or until they are cooked through and flake easily.

5 Transfer the fish to the dish with the dressing. Spoon the dressing over the fish and leave to cool completely. Cover and chill for at least 2 hours to allow the flavours to blend.

6 Transfer the sardines to a serving platter and garnish with parsley. Serve with lemon wedges for squeezing over.

Ceviche

Serves 4

INGREDIENTS

8 fresh cleaned scallops	1 lime	TO SERVE
16 large prawns in shells	1 red onion, thinly sliced	salad leaves
2 sea bass fillets, about 150 g/	½ red chilli, deseeded and	lime or lemon wedges
5½ oz each, skinned	finely chopped	pepper
1 large lemon	2–4 tbsp extra-virgin olive oil	

1 Rinse the scallops under cold running water. Cut the scallop coral free from the flesh. Slice the flesh into 2 or 3 horizontal slices each, depending on the size. Place in a non-metallic bowl with the corals.

2 Cut the heads off the prawns, then peel off the shells. Using a small sharp knife, make a thin slice all along the back of the prawns. Use the tip of the knife to remove the thin black vein. Add to the scallops.

3 Cut the sea bass fillets into thin slices across the grain and add to the shellfish.

4 Firmly roll the lemon and lime backwards and forwards on a work surface. Cut the lemon in half and squeeze the juice over the fish. Repeat with the lime.

5 Gently stir, to coat the seafood well in the citrus juices, then cover and chill for 2 hours, or until the seafood becomes opaque. Do not leave for longer because the seafood will be too soft.

6 Using a slotted spoon, transfer the seafood to a bowl. Add the onion, chilli and olive oil and gently stir together. Leave to stand for 5 minutes.

7 Spoon on to individual plates and serve with salad leaves, lemon or lime wedges and black pepper.

Crab & Celeriac Remoulade

Serves 4

INGREDIENTS

1½ tsp lemon juice	150 ml/5 fl oz extra-virgin	radicchio leaves, rinsed and dried,
1 tsp salt	olive oil	to serve
450 g/1 lb celeriac	2 tsp white wine vinegar	fresh dill or parsley sprigs,
1½ tbsp Dijon mustard	2 tbsp capers in brine, rinsed	to garnish
1 large egg yolk	300 g/10½ oz fresh crab meat	

1 Put the lemon juice and salt in a bowl of water. Using the shredding disc of a food processor or a hand grater, shred the celeriac. Put the celeriac in the bowl of acidulated water as it is grated, to prevent it from discoloring.

2 To make the sauce, beat the mustard and egg yolk together in a bowl. Gradually whisk in the olive oil, drop by drop, until a mayonnaise forms (see Cook's Tip). Stir in the white wine vinegar.

3 Drain the celeriac and pat dry with kitchen paper. Add to the mayonnaise, stirring to coat well. Cover and chill.

4 About 20 minutes before serving, remove the remoulade from the refrigerator so it can come to room temperature. Stir in the capers and crab meat.

5 Line a platter or bowl with radicchio leaves and spoon the remoulade mixture on top. Garnish with dill or parsley and serve.

COOK'S TIP

If the sauce begins to curdle, beat another egg yolk in a bowl, then slowly beat into the sauce to rectify. Continue to add the remaining oil.

Greek Salad

Serves 4

INGREDIENTS

250 g/9 oz feta cheese
250 g/9 oz cucumber
250 g/9 oz Greek kalamata olives
1 red onion or 4 spring onions

2 large juicy tomatoes
1 tsp honey
4 tbsp extra-virgin olive oil
½ lemon

salt and pepper
fresh or dried oregano, to garnish
pitta bread, to serve

1 Drain the feta cheese if it is packed in brine. Place it on a chopping board and cut into 1 cm/½ inch dice. Transfer to a salad bowl.

2 Cut the cucumber in half lengthways and use a teaspoon to scoop out the seeds. Cut the flesh into 1 cm/½ inch slices. Add to the bowl with the feta cheese.

3 Stone the olives with an olive or cherry stoner and add them to the salad bowl. Slice the red onion or finely chop the white and green parts of the spring onions, and add to the salad bowl.

4 Cut each tomato into quarters and scoop out the seeds with a teaspoon. Cut the flesh into bite-sized pieces and add to the bowl.

5 Using your hands, gently toss all the ingredients together. Stir the honey into the olive oil (see Cook's Tip), add to the salad and squeeze in lemon juice to taste. Season with pepper and a little salt, if wished. Cover and chill until required.

6 Garnish with the oregano and serve the salad with pitta bread.

COOK'S TIP

The small amount of honey helps to bring out the full flavour of the tomatoes.

Baked Goat's Cheese Salad

Serves 4

INGREDIENTS

250 g/9 oz mixed salad leaves,
such as rocket, lamb's lettuce
and chicory

DRESSING
6 tbsp extra-virgin olive oil
3 tbsp red wine vinegar

½ tsp sugar
½ tsp Dijon mustard
salt and pepper

CROUTES
12 slices French bread
extra-virgin olive oil, for brushing

12 thin slices of Provençal goat's
cheese, such as Picodon
fresh herbs, such as rosemary,
thyme or oregano,
finely chopped

extra French bread, to serve

1 To prepare the salad, rinse the leaves under cold water and pat dry with a tea towel. Wrap in kitchen paper and put in a plastic bag. Seal tightly and chill until required.

2 To make the dressing, place all the ingredients in a screw-top jar and shake until well blended. Season with salt and pepper to taste and shake again. Set aside while preparing the croûtes.

3 To make the croûtes, toast the slices of bread on both sides until they are crisp. Brush a little olive oil on one side of each slice while still hot, so the oil is absorbed.

4 Place the croûtes on a baking sheet and top each with a slice of cheese. Sprinkle the herbs over the cheese and drizzle with olive oil. Bake in a preheated oven at 180°C/350°F/Gas Mark 4 for 5 minutes.

5 While the croûtes are in the oven, place the salad leaves in a bowl. Shake the dressing again, pour it over the leaves and toss together. Divide the salad equally between 4 plates.

6 Transfer the hot croûtes to the salads. Serve at once with extra slices of French bread.

Orange & Fennel Salad

Serves 4

INGREDIENTS

4 large oranges
1 large bulb fennel
2 tsp fennel seeds

2 tbsp extra-virgin olive oil
freshly squeezed orange juice,
  to taste

finely chopped fresh parsley,
  to garnish

1 Using a small serrated knife, remove the rind and pith from one orange, cutting carefully from the top to the bottom of the orange so it retains its shape. Work over a bowl to catch the juices.

2 Peel the remaining oranges the same way, reserving all the juice. Cut horizontally into 5 mm/ ¼ inch slices and arrange in an attractive serving bowl; reserve the juices.

3 Place the fennel bulb on a chopping board and cut off the fronds. Cut the bulb in half lengthways and then

into quarters. Cut crossways into the thinnest slices you can manage. Immediately transfer to the bowl with the oranges and toss with a little of the reserved orange juice to prevent browning.

4 Sprinkle the fennel seeds evenly over the oranges and fennel.

5 Place the olive oil in a small bowl and whisk in the rest of the reserved orange juice, plus extra fresh orange juice to taste. Pour over the oranges and fennel and toss gently. Cover with cling film and chill until ready to serve.

6 Just before serving, remove from the refrigerator and sprinkle with parsley. Serve chilled.

VARIATION

Replace the fennel with a finely sliced onion or a large bunch of spring onions, finely chopped. This version is from Spain, where orange-coloured oranges would be used, but in Sicily the dish is made with blood-red oranges.

Spanish Tortilla

Serves 6–8

INGREDIENTS

125 ml/4 fl oz olive oil

600 g/1 lb 5 oz potatoes, sliced

1 large onion, sliced

1 large garlic clove, crushed

6 large eggs

salt and pepper

1 Heat a 25 cm/10 inch frying pan, preferably non-stick, over a high heat. Pour in the oil and heat. Lower the heat, add the potatoes, onion and garlic and cook for 15–20 minutes, stirring frequently, until the potatoes are tender.

2 Beat the eggs together in a large bowl and season generously with salt and pepper. Using a slotted spoon, transfer the potatoes and onion to the bowl of eggs. Pour the excess oil left in the frying pan into a heatproof jug, then scrape off the crusty bits from the base of the pan.

3 Reheat the pan. Add about 2 tablespoons of the oil reserved in the jug. Pour in the potato mixture, smoothing the vegetables into an even layer. Cook for about 5 minutes, shaking the pan occasionally, or until the base is set.

4 Shake the pan and use a spatula to loosen the edges of the tortilla. Place a large plate over the pan. Carefully invert the tortilla on to the plate.

5 If you are not using a non-stick pan, add 1 tablespoon of the reserved oil to the pan and swirl around. Gently slide the tortilla back into the pan, cooked-side up. Use the spatula to 'tuck down' the edges. Continue cooking over medium heat for 3–5 minutes until set.

6 Remove the pan from the heat and slide the tortilla on to a serving plate. Leave to stand for at least 5 minutes before cutting. Serve hot, warm or at room temperature with salad.

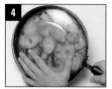

Spinach, Onion & Herb Frittata

Serves 6–8

INGREDIENTS

4 tbsp olive oil
6 spring onions, sliced
250 g/9 oz young spinach leaves,
    any coarse stems removed,
    rinsed well

6 large eggs
3 tbsp finely chopped mixed
    fresh herbs, such as flat-
    leaved parsley, thyme and
    coriander

2 tbsp freshly grated Parmesan
    cheese, plus extra for
    garnishing
salt and pepper
fresh parsley sprigs, to garnish

1 Heat a 25 cm/10 inch frying pan, preferably non-stick with a flameproof handle, over a medium heat. Add the oil and heat. Add the spring onions and fry for about 2 minutes. Add the spinach with only the water clinging to its leaves and cook until it wilts.

2 Beat the eggs together in a large bowl and season generously with salt and pepper. Using a slotted spoon, transfer the spinach and onions to the bowl of eggs and stir in the herbs. Pour the excess oil left in the frying pan into a heatproof jug, then scrape off the crusty bits from the base of the pan.

3 Reheat the pan. Add 2 tablespoons of the reserved oil. Pour in the egg mixture, smoothing it into an even layer. Cook for 6 minutes, or until the base is set when you lift up the side with a spatula, shaking the pan occasionally.

4 Sprinkle the top of the frittata with the Parmesan. Place the pan below a preheated grill and cook for about 3 minutes, or until the excess liquid is set and the cheese is golden.

5 Remove the pan from the heat and slide the tortilla on to a serving plate. Leave to stand for at least 5 minutes before cutting and garnishing with extra Parmesan and parsley. Serve hot, warm or at room temperature.

Piperade

Serves 4–6

INGREDIENTS

2 tbsp olive oil
1 large onion, finely chopped
1 large red pepper, cored, deseeded and sliced
1 large yellow pepper, cored, deseeded and sliced

1 large green pepper, cored, deseeded and sliced
8 large eggs
salt and pepper
2 tomatoes, deseeded and chopped

2 tbsp finely chopped fresh flat-leaved parsley
4–6 slices thick country-style bread, toasted, to serve
fresh flat-leaved parsley sprigs, to garnish

1 Heat the olive oil in a saucepan over a medium–high heat. Add the onion and peppers, lower the heat and cook slowly for 15–20 minutes until they are soft.

2 Meanwhile, place the eggs in a mixing bowl and whisk until well blended. Season with salt and pepper to taste. Set aside.

3 When the peppers are soft, pour the eggs into the pan and cook, stirring constantly, over a very low heat until they are almost set but still creamy. Remove from the heat.

4 Stir in the chopped tomatoes and chopped parsley. Adjust the seasoning, if necessary. Place the pieces of toast on individual plates and spoon the eggs and vegetables on top. Garnish with sprigs of parsley and serve at once.

COOK'S TIP

To make this dish more substantial, serve with thickly cut slices of Serrano ham from Spain or Parma ham from Italy. The salty taste of both contrasts well with the sweetness of the peppers.

Lemon Risotto

Serves 4

INGREDIENTS

2–3 lemons
2 tbsp olive oil
2 shallots, finely chopped
300 g/10½ oz risotto rice
125 ml/4 fl oz dry white
  vermouth

1 litre/1¾ pints vegetable or
  chicken stock, simmering
1 tbsp very, very finely chopped
  fresh flat-leaved parsley
2 tbsp butter

freshly pared Parmesan cheese
  and sliced avocado, to serve

TO GARNISH
thin strips of pared lemon zest
fresh parsley sprigs

1 Finely grate the rind from 2 lemons. Firmly roll the rindless lemons backwards and forwards on a board, then squeeze 100 ml/3½ fl oz juice. If you don't have enough, squeeze another lemon. Set the rind and juice aside.

2 Heat the olive oil in a heavy-based saucepan. Add the shallots and fry, stirring, for about 3 minutes until soft. Add the rice and stir until all the grains are well coated.

3 Stir in the vermouth and let it bubble until it evaporates. Lower the heat to medium–low. Add the lemon juice and a ladleful of simmering stock. Stir together, then leave to simmer, only stirring occasionally, until all the liquid is absorbed.

4 Add another ladleful of stock and stir, then leave to simmer until absorbed. Continue adding stock in this way, allowing it to be absorbed after each addition, until all the stock has been

used and the risotto is creamy, with several tablespoons of liquid floating on the surface.

5 Stir in the grated lemon zest and parsley. Add the butter, cover, remove from the heat and leave to stand for 5 minutes. Stir well and then garnish with lemon strips and parsley. Serve with Parmesan cheese and avocado slices.

Pissaladière

Serves 6–8

about 6 tbsp olive oil
3 large garlic cloves, crushed
1 kg/2 lb 4 oz onions,
    thinly sliced
3–4 tbsp Black Olive Tapenade
    (see page 16)
50 g/1¾ oz canned anchovy

fillets in oil, drained and
    halved lengthways
12 black olives, such as Niçoise,
    or Flavoured Olives (see page
    172), stoned
finely chopped fresh flat-leaved
    parsley, to garnish

CRUST
175 g/6 oz plain flour
pinch of salt
85 g/3 oz butter, diced
2–3 tbsp ice-cold water

1 To make the pastry crust, put the flour and salt in a bowl; stir. With your fingertips, rub the butter into the flour until fine crumbs form. Add 2 tablespoons of the water to make a dough. Only add the extra water if necessary. Lightly knead the dough, then shape into a ball, wrap in clingfilm and chill for at least 1 hour.

2 Heat the oil in a large frying pan with a tight-fitting lid. Add the garlic and stir for 2 minutes. Add the onions and stir to coat in oil.

Turn the heat down to its lowest setting.

3 Dip a piece of baking parchment, large enough to fit over the top of the pan, in water. Shake off the excess and press it on to the onions. Cover with the lid and cook for 45 minutes, or until the onions are tender.

4 Meanwhile, roll out the dough on a lightly floured surface and use to line a 20 cm/8 inch tart tin with a removable base. Prick all over and line with baking

parchment and baking beans. Chill for 10 minutes.

5 Bake the lined pastry shell on a hot baking sheet in a preheated oven at 220°C/425°F/Gas Mark 7 for 15 minutes. Remove the paper and bake for a further 5 minutes. Lower the oven to 180°C/350°F/Gas Mark 4.

6 Spread the tapenade over the baked pastry shell. Fill the shell with the onions. Arrange the anchovy fillets in a lattice pattern and scatter the olives over the top.

7 Bake for 25–30 minutes. Stand for 10 minutes before removing from the tin. Scatter with the parsley and serve.

Spanakopittas

Serves 4

INGREDIENTS

2 tbsp olive oil

6 spring onions, chopped

250 g/9 oz fresh young spinach
    leaves, tough stems removed,
    rinsed well

60 g/2¼ oz long-grain rice (not
    basmati), boiled until tender
    and drained

4 tbsp chopped fresh dill

4 tbsp chopped fresh parsley

4 tbsp pine kernels

2 tbsp raisins

60 g/2¼ oz feta cheese, drained if
    necessary and cubed

1 nutmeg

pinch of cayenne pepper
    (optional)

40 sheets filo pastry

about 250 g/9 oz melted butter

black pepper

1 Heat the oil in a pan, add the spring onions and fry for about 2 minutes. Add the spinach, with just the water clinging to the leaves, and cook, stirring, until the leaves wilt. Squeeze excess moisture out of the spinach, using a wooden spoon.

2 Stir in the rice, herbs, pine kernels, raisins and feta cheese. Grate in one-quarter of the nutmeg, and add black and cayenne peppers to taste.

3 Leave the filo sheets in a stack. Cut forty 15 cm/ 6 inch squares. Remove eight squares and cut into eight 10 cm/4 inch circles. Re-wrap the unused pastry and cover the squares and circles with a damp tea towel.

4 Brush a 10 cm/4 inch tart tin with a removable base with butter. Place in one square of filo and brush with more butter. Repeat with 7 more squares. Do not push the filo into the ridges.

5 Spoon in one-quarter of the filling and smooth the surface. Top with a filo circle and brush with butter. Repeat with another filo circle. Fold the overhanging filo over the top and brush with butter. Make 3 more pies.

6 Put the pies on a baking sheet and bake in a preheated oven at 180°C/350°F/Gas Mark 4 for 20–25 minutes until crisp and golden. Leave to stand for 5 minutes before turning out.

Tuna & Tomato Boreks

Makes about 18 boreks

INGREDIENTS

about 18 sheets filo pastry, each
45 x 15 cm/15 x 6 inches,
defrosted if frozen
vegetable oil, for shallow frying
sea salt, to garnish
lemon wedges, to serve

FILLING
2 hard-boiled eggs, shelled
and finely chopped
200 g/7 oz canned tuna in
brine, drained

1 tbsp chopped fresh dill
1 tomato, skinned, deseeded and
very finely chopped
¼ tsp cayenne pepper
salt and pepper

1 To make the filling, put the eggs in a bowl with the tuna and dill and mash the mixture until blended.

2 Stir in the tomato, taking care not to break it up too much. Season with the cayenne and salt and pepper to taste. Set aside.

3 Place one sheet of filo pastry on the work surface with a short side nearest to you; keep the remaining sheets covered with a damp tea towel.

Arrange about 1 tablespoon of the filling in a line along the short side, about 1 cm/½ inch in from the end and 2.5 cm/1 inch in from both long sides.

4 Make one tight roll to enclose the filling, then fold in both long sides for the length of the filo pastry. Continue rolling up to the end. Use a little vegetable oil to seal the end. Repeat the sequence to make 17 more rolls, or until all the filling has been used up.

5 Heat 2.5 cm/1 inch oil in a frying pan to 180–190°C/350–375°F, or until a cube of day-old bread browns in 30 seconds. Fry 2–3 boreks at a time, until they are golden brown all over. Drain well on crumpled kitchen paper and sprinkle with sea salt. Serve hot or at room temperature with lemon wedges.

Pizza Biancas with Courgettes

Makes two 23 cm / 9 inch pizzas

INGREDIENTS

400 g/14 oz plain flour, plus extra
    for rolling and dusting
1 sachet easy-blend dried yeast

1 tsp salt
1 tbsp extra-virgin olive oil, plus
    extra for greasing

TOPPING
2 courgettes
300 g/10½ oz buffalo mozzarella
1½–2 tbsp finely chopped fresh
    rosemary, or ½ tbsp dried

1 To make the crust, heat 225 ml/ 8 fl oz water in the microwave on High for 1 minute, or until it reads 52°C/125°F on an instant-read thermometer.

2 Stir the flour, yeast and salt together and make a well in the centre. Stir in most of the water with the olive oil to make a dough. Add the remaining water, if necessary, to form a soft dough.

3 Turn out on to a lightly floured surface and knead for about 10 minutes until smooth but still soft. Wash the bowl and lightly coat with olive oil. Shape the dough into a ball, put it in the bowl and turn the dough over so it is coated. Cover and leave until doubled in size.

4 Turn the dough out on to a lightly floured surface. Quickly knead a few times, then cover with the upturned bowl and leave to rest for 10 minutes.

5 Meanwhile, using a vegetable peeler, cut long, thin strips of courgettes. Drain and dice the mozzarella.

6 Divide the dough in half and shape each half into a ball. Cover one ball and roll out the other one into a 23 cm/9 inch round. Place the round on a lightly floured baking sheet.

7 Scatter half the mozzarella over the base. Add half the courgette strips and sprinkle with half the rosemary. Repeat with the remaining dough.

8 Bake in a preheated oven at 220°C/425°F/Gas Mark 7 for 15 minutes, or until crispy.

Pan Bagna

Serves 4

INGREDIENTS

40 cm/16 inch long loaf of
country bread, thicker than
a French baguette
fruity extra-virgin olive oil
Black or Green Olive Tapenade
(see page 16), optional

FILLING
2 eggs
50 g/1¾ oz canned anchovy
fillets in oil
about 85 g/3 oz Flavoured Olives
of your choice (see page 172)

lettuce or rocket leaves, rinsed
and patted dry
about 4 plum tomatoes, sliced
200 g/7 oz canned tuna in brine,
well drained and flaked

1 To make the filling, start by hard-boiling the eggs. Bring a saucepan of water to the boil. Add the eggs and return the water to the boil, then continue boiling for 12 minutes. Drain and immediately plunge into a bowl of ice-cold water to stop the cooking.

2 Shell the cooked eggs and cut into slices. Drain the anchovy fillets well, then cut them in half lengthways if large. Stone the olives and slice in half. Set aside.

3 Using a serrated knife, slice the loaf in half lengthways. Remove about 1 cm/½ inch of the crumb from the top and bottom pieces, leaving a border all around both halves.

4 Generously brush both halves with the olive oil. Spread with tapenade, if you like a strong, robust flavour. Arrange a layer of lettuce or rocket leaves on the bottom half.

5 Add layers of hard-boiled egg slices, tomato slices,

olives, anchovies and tuna, sprinkling with olive oil and adding lettuce or rocket leaves between the layers. Make the filling as thick as you like.

6 Place the other bread half on top and press down firmly. Wrap tightly in clingfilm and place on a board or plate that will fit in your refrigerator. Weight down and chill for several hours. To serve, slice into 4 equal portions, tying with string to secure in place, if wished.

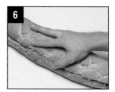

Olive Cake

Makes 12–15 slices

INGREDIENTS

250 g/9 oz stoned black or green olives, or a mixture	4 large eggs	125 ml/4 fl oz olive oil
300 g/10½ oz self-raising flour	1 tbsp caster sugar	butter, for greasing
	125 ml/4 fl oz milk	salt and pepper

1 Lightly butter a 20 cm/8 inch cake tin, 5 cm/2 inches deep. Line the base with a piece of baking parchment cut to fit. Put the olives in a small bowl and toss in 2 tablespoons of the measured flour.

2 Break the eggs into a bowl and lightly whisk. Stir in the sugar and season with salt and pepper to taste. Stir in the milk and olive oil.

3 Sift the remaining flour into the bowl, add the coated olives and stir together. Spoon the mixture into the prepared tin and smooth the surface.

4 Bake in a preheated oven at 200°C/400°F/Gas Mark 6 for 45 minutes. Lower the oven temperature to 160°C/325°F/Gas Mark 3 and continue baking for 15 minutes until the cake is risen, golden and coming away from the side of the tin.

5 Remove from the oven and leave to cool in the tin on a wire rack for 20 minutes. Remove from the tin, peel off the lining paper and leave to cool completely. Store the cake in an airtight container.

COOK'S TIP

Serve this with Black Olive Tapenade (see page 16) for spreading, or as part of an antipasti platter with a selection of cooked meats.

Main Courses

The seemingly endless variety of fish and shellfish from Mediterranean waters means Mediterranean cooks can rely on freshly caught ingredients in the best condition. Mouthwatering dishes combining shellfish and fish are a speciality and the Seafood Stew is a classic example. For a taste of heartier Mediterranean flavours, try Seared Tuna with Anchovy & Orange Butter, or pan-fried red mullet wrapped in vine leaves. Few dishes can be easier to prepare than Mediterranean Monkfish, where the sweet white fish is paired with cherry tomatoes and pesto sauce.

The Italians love their tender veal – Vitello Tonnato is a divine combination of veal and tuna – while the Greeks, Turks and Moroccans always cook lamb, often grilled with herbs. Pork is often turned into hearty dishes, transforming the most inexpensive cuts into succulent meals, such as Country Pork with Onions. Mediterranean winters can be as cold and fierce as the summers are hot, so comforting casseroles are also called for. When you need a one-pot dinner to take the chill off a grey winter day, try Traditional Provençal Daube, Moroccan Chicken Couscous or Basque Pork & Beans.

Traditional Provençal Daube

Serves 4

INGREDIENTS

700 g/1 lb 9 oz boneless lean
stewing beef, such as leg, cut
into 5 cm/2 inch pieces

400 ml/14 fl oz full-bodied dry
red wine

2 tbsp olive oil

4 large garlic cloves, crushed

4 shallots, thinly sliced

250 g/9 oz unsmoked lardons or
bacon pieces, diced

5–6 tbsp plain flour

250 g/9 oz large chestnut
mushrooms, sliced

400 g/14 oz canned chopped
tomatoes

1 bouquet garni of 1 bay leaf,
2 sprigs dried thyme and
2 sprigs fresh parsley, tied in
a small piece of celery

5 cm/2 inch strip dried orange
rind (see page 176, optional)

450 ml/16 fl oz oz beef stock

50 g/1¾ oz canned anchovy
fillets in oil

2 tbsp capers in brine, drained

2 tbsp red wine vinegar

2 tbsp finely chopped fresh
parsley

salt and pepper

1 Place the stewing beef in a non-metallic bowl with the wine, olive oil, half the garlic and the shallots. Cover and leave to marinate for at least 4 hours, stirring from time to time.

2 Meanwhile, place the lardons in a pan of water, bring to the boil and simmer for 10 minutes. Drain.

3 Place 4 tablespoons of the flour in a bowl and stir in about 2 tablespoons water to make a thick paste. Cover and set aside.

4 Strain the marinated beef, reserving the marinade. Pat the beef dry and toss in seasoned flour.

5 Arrange a layer of lardons, mushrooms and tomatoes in a large flameproof casserole, then add a layer of beef. Continue layering until all the ingredients are used, tucking in the bouquet garni and orange rind, if using.

6 Pour in the beef stock and reserved marinade. Spread the flour paste around the rim of the casserole. Press on the lid, sealing tightly.

7 Cook in a preheated oven at 160°C/325°F/ Gas Mark 3 for 2½ hours. Drain the anchovies, then pound with the capers and remaining garlic.

8 Remove the casserole, break the seal and stir in the anchovies, vinegar and parsley. Cover and cook for a further 1–1½ hours until the meat is tender.

Vitello Tonnato

Serves 6–8

INGREDIENTS

1 boned and rolled piece of
    veal leg, about 900 g/2 lb
    boned weight
olive oil
salt and pepper

TUNA MAYONNAISE
150 g/5½ oz canned tuna in
    olive oil
2 large eggs
about 3 tbsp lemon juice
olive oil

TO GARNISH
8 black olives, stoned and halved
1 tbsp capers in brine, rinsed
    and drained
finely chopped fresh flat-leaved
    parsley
lemon wedges

1 Rub the veal all over with oil and pepper and place in a roasting tin. Cover the meat with a piece of foil if there isn't any fat on it, then roast in a preheated oven at 230°C/450°F/Gas Mark 8 for 10 minutes. Lower the heat to 180°C/350°F/Gas Mark 4 and continue roasting for 1 hour for medium, or 1¼ hours for well-done. Set the veal aside and leave to cool completely, reserving any juices in the roasting tin.

2 Meanwhile, drain the tuna, reserving the oil. Blend the eggs in a food processor with 1 teaspoon of the lemon juice and a pinch of salt. Add enough olive oil to the tuna oil to make up to 300 ml/10 fl oz.

3 With the motor running, add the oil to the eggs, drop by drop, until a thin mayonnaise forms. Add the tuna and process until smooth. Blend in lemon juice to taste. Check and adjust the seasoning.

4 Slice the cool meat very thinly. Add any juices to the reserved pan juices. Gradually whisk the veal juices into the tuna mayonnaise, to obtain a thin, pouring consistency.

5 Layer the veal slices with the sauce on a platter, ending with a layer of sauce. Cover and leave to chill overnight. Garnish with olives, capers and a light sprinkling of parsley. Arrange lemon wedges around the edge and serve.

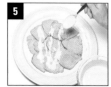

Veal Chops with Salsa Verde

Serves 4

INGREDIENTS

4 veal chops, such as loin chops, about 225 g/8 oz each and 2 cm/¾ inch thick	SALSA VERDE	1 garlic clove, halved, green core removed and chopped
garlic-flavoured olive oil, for brushing	60 g/2¼ oz fresh flat-leaved parsley	1 tbsp lemon juice, or to taste
salt and pepper	3 canned anchovy fillets in oil, drained	6 large fresh basil leaves, or ¾ tsp freeze-dried
fresh basil or oregano leaves, to garnish	½ tbsp capers in brine, rinsed and drained	2 sprigs fresh oregano, or ½ tsp dried
	1 shallot, finely chopped	125 ml/4 fl oz extra-virgin olive oil

1 To make the salsa verde, put all the ingredients, except the olive oil, in a blender or food processor and process until they are chopped and blended.

2 With the motor running, add the oil through the top or feed tube and quickly blend until thickened. Add pepper to taste. Transfer to a bowl, cover and chill.

3 Take the garlic-flavoured olive oil and lightly brush it over the veal chops. Season them with salt and pepper. Place them under a preheated grill and cook for about 3 minutes. Turn over, brush with more oil and grill for a further 2 minutes until cooked. Use the tip of a knife to test they are cooked.

4 Transfer the chops to individual plates and spoon a little of the chilled salsa verde alongside them. Garnish the chops with fresh basil or oregano and serve with the remaining salsa verde handed separately.

COOK'S TIP

The salsa verde will keep for up to 2 days in a covered container in the refrigerator. It is also delicious served with grilled red mullet. Or use it to replace the pesto sauce in Mediterranean Monkfish (see page 108).

Osso Bucco with Citrus Rinds

Serves 6

INGREDIENTS

1–2 tbsp plain flour

6 meaty slices osso bucco
(veal shins)

1 kg/2 lb 4 oz fresh tomatoes,
skinned, deseeded and diced,
or 800 g/1 lb 12oz canned
chopped tomatoes

1–2 tbsp olive oil

250 g/9 oz onions, very
finely chopped

250 g/9 oz carrots, finely diced

225 ml/8 fl oz dry white wine

225 ml/8 fl oz veal stock

6 large basil leaves, torn

1 large garlic clove, very
finely chopped

finely grated rind of
1 large lemon

finely grated rind of 1 orange

2 tbsp finely chopped fresh
flat-leaved parsley

salt and pepper

1 Put the flour in a plastic bag and season with salt and pepper. Add the osso bucco, a couple of pieces at a time, and shake until well coated. Remove and shake off the excess flour. Continue until all the pieces are coated.

2 If using canned tomatoes, put them in a sieve and leave to drain.

3 Heat 1 tablespoon of the oil in a large flameproof casserole. Add the osso bucco and fry for 10 minutes on each side until well browned. Remove from the pan.

4 Add 1–2 teaspoons oil to the casserole if necessary. Add the onions and fry for about 5 minutes, stirring, until soft. Stir in the carrots and continue frying until they become soft.

5 Add the tomatoes, wine, stock and basil and return the osso bucco to the pan. Bring to the boil, then lower the heat and simmer for 1 hour, covered. Check that the meat is tender with the tip of a knife. If not, continue cooking for 10 minutes and test again.

6 When the meat is tender, sprinkle with the garlic and lemon and orange rinds, re-cover and cook for a further 10 minutes.

7 Adjust the seasoning, if necessary. Sprinkle with the parsley and serve.

Spanish Chicken with Garlic

Serves 4

INGREDIENTS

2–3 tbsp plain flour	salt and pepper	1 large bay leaf
cayenne pepper	about 4 tbsp olive oil	450 ml/16 fl oz chicken stock
4 chicken quarters or other joints, patted dry	20 large garlic cloves, each halved and green core removed	4 tbsp dry white wine
		chopped fresh parsley, to garnish

1 Put about 2 tablespoons of the flour in a bag and season to taste with cayenne pepper and salt and pepper. Add a chicken piece and shake until it is lightly coated with the flour, shaking off the excess. Repeat with the remaining pieces, adding more flour and seasoning, if necessary.

2 Heat 3 tablespoons of the olive oil in a large frying pan. Add the garlic cloves and fry for about 2 minutes, stirring, to flavour the oil. Remove the garlic with a slotted spoon and set aside.

3 Add the chicken pieces to the pan, skin-side down, and fry for 5 minutes, or until the skin is golden brown. Turn and fry for a further 5 minutes, adding an extra 1–2 tablespoons of oil if necessary.

4 Return the garlic to the pan. Add the bay leaf, chicken stock and wine and bring to the boil. Lower the heat, cover and simmer for 25 minutes, or until the chicken is tender and the garlic cloves are very soft.

5 Using a slotted spoon, transfer the chicken to a serving platter and keep warm. Bring the cooking liquid to the boil, with the garlic, and boil until reduced to about 250 ml/9 fl oz. Adjust the seasoning.

6 Spoon the sauce over the chicken pieces and scatter the garlic cloves around. Garnish with parsley and serve.

COOK'S TIP

The cooked garlic cloves are delicious mashed and smeared on the chicken pieces.

Moroccan Chicken Couscous

Serves 4–6

INGREDIENTS

about 3 tbsp olive oil

8 chicken pieces with bones, such as quarters, breasts and legs

2 large onions, chopped

2 large garlic cloves, crushed

2.5 cm/1 inch piece fresh root ginger, peeled and finely chopped

150 g/5½ oz dried chickpeas, soaked overnight and drained

4 large carrots, cut into thick chunks

large pinch of saffron threads, dissolved in 2 tbsp boiling water

finely grated rind of 2 lemons

2 red peppers, cored, deseeded and sliced

2 large courgettes, cut into chunks

2 tomatoes, cored, deseeded and chopped

100 g/3½ oz dried apricots, chopped

½ tsp ground cumin

½ tsp ground coriander

½ tsp cayenne pepper, or to taste

600 ml/1 pint water

15 g/½ oz butter

600 g/1 lb 5 oz instant couscous

salt and pepper

harissa, to serve (optional)

1 Heat 3 tablespoons of the oil in a large flameproof casserole. Pat the chicken pieces dry with kitchen paper, add to the oil, skin-side down, and cook for 5 minutes until brown. Remove from the pan and set aside.

2 Add the onions to the pan, with a little more oil, if necessary. Fry for 5 minutes, then add the garlic and ginger and cook for 2 minutes.

3 Return the chicken to the casserole. Add the chickpeas, carrots, saffron and lemon rind. Cover with 2.5 cm/1 inch of water. Bring to the boil.

4 Lower the heat, cover and simmer for 45 minutes, or until the chickpeas are tender. Add the peppers, courgettes, tomatoes, dried apricots, cumin, coriander, cayenne pepper, and salt and pepper to taste. Re-cover and simmer for a further 15 minutes.

5 Meanwhile, bring the water to the boil. Stir in ½ teaspoon salt and the butter. Sprinkle in the couscous. Cover the pan tightly, remove from the heat and leave for about 10 minutes.

6 Fluff the couscous with a fork. Spoon the couscous into individual bowls and serve the stew and harissa, if using, separately.

Provençal Barbecued Lamb

Serves 4–6

INGREDIENTS

1 leg of lamb, about 1.5 kg/
    3 lb 5 oz, boned
about 1 quantity Black Olive
    Tapenade (see page 16)
olive oil, for brushing

fresh rosemary and thyme sprigs,
    to garnish

MARINADE
1 bottle full-bodied red wine

2 large garlic cloves, chopped
2 tbsp extra-virgin olive oil
large handful fresh
    rosemary sprigs
fresh thyme sprigs

1 Place the boned lamb on a chopping board. Holding the knife almost flat, slice horizontally into the pocket left by the leg bone, taking care not to cut all the way through, so the boned meat can be opened out flat, like a book.

2 Place the lamb in a large non-metallic bowl and add all the marinade ingredients. Cover with clingfilm and leave to marinate for at least 6 hours, but preferably up to 24 hours, turning the meat over several times.

3 When ready to cook, remove the lamb from the marinade and pat dry. Lay the lamb flat and thread 2 or 3 long metal skewers through the flesh, so that the meat remains flat while it cooks. Spread the tapenade all over the lamb on both sides.

4 Brush the barbecue rack with oil. Place the lamb on the rack about 10 cm/ 4 inch inches above hot coals and cook for 5 minutes. Turn the meat over, and continue cooking for about 5 minutes longer. Turn twice more at 5-minute intervals, brushing

with extra tapenade. Raise the rack to 15 cm/6 inches if the meat starts to look charred – it should be medium cooked after 20–25 minutes.

5 Remove the lamb from the heat and leave to stand for 10 minutes before carving into thin slices and serving, garnished with rosemary and thyme sprigs.

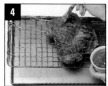

Lamb Skewers on Rosemary

Makes 4

INGREDIENTS

500 g/1 lb 2 oz boneless leg of lamb	12 large garlic cloves, peeled olive oil	MARINADE
4 long, thick branches fresh rosemary	Spiced Pilau with Saffron (see page 196), to serve	2 tbsp olive oil
1 or 2 red peppers		2 tbsp dry white wine
		½ tsp ground cumin
		1 sprig fresh oregano, chopped

1 At least 4 hours before cooking, cut the lamb into 5 cm/2 inch cubes. Mix all the marinade ingredients together in a bowl. Add the lamb cubes, stir well to coat and leave to marinate for at least 4 hours, or up to 12.

2 An hour before cooking, put the rosemary in a bowl of cold water and leave it to soak.

3 Slice the tops off the peppers, cut the peppers in half, quarter them and remove the cores and seeds. Now cut the halves into pieces about 5 cm/2 inches in size.

4 Bring a small saucepan of water to the boil, blanch the pepper pieces and garlic cloves for 1 minute. Drain and refresh under cold water. Pat dry and set aside.

5 Remove the rosemary from the water and pat dry. To make the skewers, remove the needles from about the first 4 cm/1½ inches of the branches so you have a 'handle' to turn them over with while grilling.

6 Thread alternate pieces of lamb, garlic and red pepper pieces on to the 4 rosemary skewers: the meat should be tender enough to push the sprig through it, but, if not, use a metal skewer to poke a hole in the centre of each cube.

7 Lightly oil the grill rack. Place the skewers on the rack about 13 cm/5 inches under a preheated hot grill and grill for 10–12 minutes, brushing with any leftover marinade or olive oil and turning, until the meat is cooked. Serve with the pilau.

Cypriot Lamb with Orzo

Serves 6

INGREDIENTS

2 large garlic cloves	4 sprigs fresh thyme	250 g/9 oz orzo pasta
1 unboned shoulder of lamb	4 sprigs fresh parsley	(see Cook's Tip)
800 g/1 lb 12 oz canned chopped	1 bay leaf	salt and pepper
tomatoes	125 ml/4 fl oz water	fresh thyme sprigs, to garnish

1 Cut the garlic cloves in half and remove the green cores, then thinly slice. Using the tip of a sharp knife, make slits all over the lamb shoulder, then insert the garlic slices into the slits.

2 Tip the tomatoes and their juices into a roasting tin large enough to hold the lamb shoulder. Add the thyme, parsley and bay leaf. Place the lamb on top, skin-side up, and cover the dish tightly with a sheet of foil, shiny side down. Scrunch the foil all around the edge so that none of the juices escape during cooking.

3 Put in a preheated oven at 160°C/325°F/Gas Mark 3 and cook for about 3½–4 hours until the lamb is really tender and the tomatoes are reduced to a thick sauce.

4 Remove the lamb from the roasting tin and set aside. Using a large metal spoon, skim off as much fat from the surface of the tomato sauce as possible.

5 Add the water and orzo to the tomatoes, stirring so the grains are submerged. Add a little extra water if the sauce seems too thick. Season to taste with salt and

pepper. Return the lamb to the roasting tin.

6 Re-cover the roasting tin and return to the oven for 15 minutes, or until the orzo is tender. Remove the bay leaf. Leave the lamb to rest for 10 minutes, then slice and serve with the orzo in tomato juice, garnished with fresh thyme sprigs.

COOK'S TIP

Orzo is a small pasta shape that looks like barley grains.

Basque Pork & Beans

Serves 4–6

INGREDIENTS

200 g/7 oz dried cannellini beans,
    soaked overnight
olive oil
600 g/1 lb 5 oz boneless leg of
    pork, cut into 5 cm/2 inch
    chunks

1 large onion, sliced
3 large garlic cloves, crushed
400 g/14 oz canned
    chopped tomatoes
2 green peppers, cored, deseeded
    and sliced

finely grated rind of
    1 large orange
salt and pepper
finely chopped fresh parsley,
    to garnish

1 Drain the cannellini beans and put in a large saucepan with fresh water to cover. Bring to the boil and boil rapidly for 10 minutes. Lower the heat and simmer for 20 minutes. Drain the beans and set aside.

2 Add enough oil to cover the base of a frying pan in a very thin layer. Heat the oil over medium heat, add a few pieces of the pork and fry on all sides until brown. Repeat with the remaining pork and set aside.

3 Add 1 tablespoon oil to the frying pan, if necessary, then add the onion and fry for 3 minutes. Stir in the garlic and fry for a further 2 minutes. Return the browned pork to the pan.

4 Add the tomatoes to the pan and bring to the boil. Lower the heat, stir in the pepper slices, orange rind, the drained beans and salt and pepper to taste.

5 Transfer the contents of the pan to a casserole.

6 Cover the casserole and cook in a preheated oven at 180°C/350°F/Gas Mark 4 for 45 minutes, until the beans and pork are tender. Sprinkle with parsley and serve.

VARIATION

Any leftover beans and peppers can be used as a pasta sauce. Add some sliced and fried chorizo sausage for a spicier dish.

Country Pork with Onions

Serves 4

INGREDIENTS

2 large pork shanks
2 large garlic cloves, sliced
3 tbsp olive oil
2 carrots, finely chopped
2 celery stalks, strings removed and finely chopped

1 large onion, finely chopped
2 sprigs fresh thyme, broken into pieces
2 sprigs fresh rosemary, broken into pieces
1 large bay leaf

225 ml/8 fl oz dry white wine
225 ml/8 fl oz water
20 pickling onions
pepper
roughly chopped fresh flat-leaved parsley, to garnish

1 Using the tip of a sharp knife, make slits all over the pork shanks and insert the garlic slices.

2 Heat 1 tablespoon of the oil in a flameproof casserole over a medium heat. Add the carrots, celery and onion and fry, stirring occasionally, for about 10 minutes.

3 Place the pork shanks on top of the vegetables. Scatter the thyme and rosemary over the meat. Add the bay leaf, wine and water and season with pepper.

4 Bring to the boil, then remove from the heat. Cover tightly and cook in a preheated oven at 160°C/325°F/Gas Mark 3 for 3½ hours, or until the meat is very tender.

5 Meanwhile, put the onions in a bowl, pour over boiling water and leave for 1 minute. Drain, then slip off all the skins. Heat the remaining oil in a large frying pan. Add the onions, partially cover and cook over a low heat for 15 minutes, shaking the pan occasionally, until the

onions are just starting to turn golden.

6 When the pork shanks are tender, add the onions and cook for a further 15 minutes. Remove the pork and onions and keep warm.

7 Using a large metal spoon, skim off as much fat as possible from the surface of the cooking liquid. Strain the cooking liquid into a bowl, pressing down lightly to extract the flavour; reserve the strained vegetables in the strainer. Adjust the seasoning.

8 Cut the meat from the pork shanks, if wished. Arrange on a serving platter with the onions and strained vegetables. Spoon the sauce over the meat and vegetables. Garnish with parsley.

Maltese Rabbit with Fennel

Serves 4

INGREDIENTS

5 tbsp olive oil

2 large fennel bulbs, trimmed
and sliced

2 carrots, diced

1 large garlic clove, crushed

1 tbsp fennel seeds

about 4 tbsp plain flour

2 wild rabbits, jointed

225 ml/8 fl oz dry white wine

225 ml/8 fl oz water

1 bouquet garni of 2 sprigs fresh
flat-leaved parsley, 1 sprig fresh
rosemary and 1 bay leaf, tied in
a 7.5 cm/3 inch piece of celery

salt and pepper

thick, crusty bread, to serve

TO GARNISH

finely chopped fresh flat-leaved
parsley or coriander

fresh rosemary sprigs

1 Heat 3 tablespoons of the olive oil over a medium heat in a large flameproof casserole. Add the fennel and carrots and cook for 5 minutes, stirring occasionally. Stir in the garlic and fennel seeds and continue to cook for 2 minutes, or until the fennel is tender. Remove the fennel and carrots from the casserole and set aside.

2 Put 4 tablespoons flour in a plastic bag and season. Add 2 rabbit pieces and shake to coat lightly, then shake off any excess flour. Continue until all the pieces of rabbit are coated, adding more flour, if necessary.

3 Add the remaining oil to the casserole. Fry the rabbit pieces for about 5 minutes on each side until golden brown, working in batches. Remove the rabbit from the casserole as it is cooked and set aside.

4 Pour in the wine and bubble over heat, stirring to scrape up all the bits from the bottom. Return the rabbit pieces, fennel and carrots to the casserole and pour in the water. Add the bouquet garni and salt and pepper to taste.

5 Bring to the boil. Lower the heat, cover and simmer for about 1¼ hours until the rabbit is tender.

6 Discard the bouquet garni. Garnish with herbs and serve straight from the casserole with lots of bread to mop up the juices.

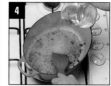

Pickled Tuna

Serves 4

INGREDIENTS

4 large tuna steaks, each 225 g/ 8 oz and 2 cm/¾ inch thick 225 ml/8 fl oz olive oil 2 large red onions, thinly sliced 2 carrots, thinly sliced 2 large bay leaves, torn	1 garlic clove, very finely chopped 225 ml/8 fl oz white wine vinegar or sherry vinegar ½ tsp dried chilli flakes, or to taste, crushed	1 tbsp coriander seeds, lightly crushed salt and pepper finely chopped fresh parsley, to garnish

1 Rinse and pat the tuna steaks dry with kitchen paper. Heat 4 tablespoons of the oil in a large frying pan, preferably non-stick.

2 Add the tuna steaks to the pan and fry for 2 minutes over a medium–high heat. Turn the steaks and continue to cook for 2 minutes, until browned and medium cooked, or 4 minutes for well done. Remove the tuna from the pan and drain well on kitchen paper. Set aside.

3 Heat the remaining oil in the pan. Add the onions and cook for 8 minutes, stirring frequently, until soft but not brown. Stir in the carrots, bay leaves, garlic, vinegar, dried chilli flakes and salt and pepper to taste and cook for 10 minutes, or until the carrots are tender. Stir in the coriander seeds 1 minute before the end of cooking.

4 When the tuna steaks are cool enough to be handled easily, remove any skin and bones from them.

Break each of the steaks into 4 or 5 large chunks.

5 Put the fish pieces in a non-metallic bowl and pour the hot onion mixture over. Very gently mix together, taking care not to break up the fish pieces.

6 Leave until completely cool, then cover and chill for at least 24 hours: the fish will stay fresh in the refrigerator for up to 5 days. Sprinkle with parsley and serve at room temperature.

Seared Tuna with Anchovy & Orange Butter

Serves 4

INGREDIENTS

olive oil
4 thick tuna steaks, each
    about 225 g/8 oz and
    2 cm/¾ inch thick

ANCHOVY AND ORANGE BUTTER
8 anchovy fillets in oil, drained
4 spring onions, finely chopped
1 tbsp finely grated orange rind
115 g/4 oz unsalted butter
¼ tsp lemon juice
pepper

TO GARNISH
fresh flat-leaved parsley sprigs
orange rind strips

1 To make the anchovy and orange butter, very finely chop the anchovies and put them in a bowl with the spring onions, orange rind and softened butter. Beat until all the ingredients are blended together, seasoning with lemon juice and pepper to taste.

2 Place the flavoured butter on a sheet of baking parchment and roll up into a log shape. Fold over the ends and place in the freezer for 15 minutes to allow it to become firm.

3 To cook the tuna, heat a ridged frying pan over a high heat. Lightly brush the pan with olive oil, add the tuna steaks, in batches if necessary, and fry for 2 minutes. Turn the steaks over and fry for 2 minutes for rare, or up to 4 minutes for well done. Season to taste with salt and pepper.

4 Transfer to a warm plate and put 2 thin slices of anchovy butter on each tuna steak. Garnish with parsley sprigs and orange rind and serve at once.

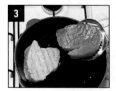

Mediterranean Fish Soup

Serves 4

INGREDIENTS

1 kg/2 lb 4 oz mixed fish, such as sea bass, skate, red snapper, rock fish or any Mediterranean fish
2 tbsp olive oil
1 bulb fennel, trimmed and chopped
2 shallots, chopped
2 garlic cloves, chopped
600 g/1 lb 5 oz vine-ripened tomatoes, chopped

1 bouquet garni of 2 sprigs fresh flat-leaved parsley, 2 sprigs fresh thyme and 1 bay leaf, tied in a 7.5 cm/3 inch piece of celery
pinch of saffron threads
700 ml/1¼ pints Mediterranean Fish Stock (see page 180), or good-quality, ready-made chilled fish stock
salt and pepper

French pastis or other aniseed-flavoured liqueur (optional)

TO SERVE
Rouille (see page 186)
1 loaf French bread, sliced and toasted
125 g/4½ oz Gruyère cheese, grated

1 To prepare the fish, remove any skin and bones and cut into pieces.

2 Heat the oil in a heavy-based pan. Add the fennel and cook for 5 minutes. Stir frequently. Add the shallots and garlic and cook for about 5 minutes until the fennel is tender.

3 Stir in the mixed fish and add the tomatoes, bouquet garni, saffron, fish stock and salt and pepper to taste.

4 Slowly bring almost to the boil, stirring occasionally. Lower the heat, partially cover and simmer for 30 minutes, stirring occasionally to break up the tomatoes. Skim the surface as necessary.

5 Remove the bouquet garni. Process the soup in a food processor, then work it through a food mill into a large bowl.

6 Return to the rinsed-out pan and heat without boiling. Adjust the seasoning. Stir in a little pastis, if using.

7 Spread the rouille on the toast and top with the cheese. Place in each bowl and ladle over the hot soup. Serve at once.

Seafood Stew

Serves 4–6

INGREDIENTS

225 g/8 oz clams

700 g/1 lb 9 oz mixed fish, such
as sea bass, skate, red
snapper, rock fish or
any Mediterranean fish you
can find

12–18 tiger prawns

about 3 tbsp olive oil

1 large onion, finely chopped

2 garlic cloves, very finely
chopped

2 vine-ripened tomatoes, halved,
deseeded and chopped

700 ml/1¼ pints Mediterranean
Fish Stock (see page 180), or
good-quality, ready-made
chilled fish stock

1 tbsp tomato purée

1 tsp fresh thyme leaves

pinch of saffron threads

pinch of sugar

salt and pepper

finely chopped fresh parsley,
to garnish

1 Leave the clams to soak in a bowl of lightly salted water for 30 minutes. Rinse them under cold running water and lightly scrub to remove any sand from the shells. Discard any broken clams or open clams that do not shut when firmly tapped with the back of a knife as these will be unsafe to eat.

2 Prepare the fish as necessary, removing any skin and bones, then cut into bite-sized chunks.

3 To prepare the prawns, break off the heads. Peel off the shells, leaving the tails intact, if wished. Using a small knife, make a slit along the back of each and remove the thin black vein. Set all the seafood aside.

4 Heat the oil in a large pan. Add the onion and fry for 5 minutes, stirring. Add the garlic and fry for about another 2 minutes until the onion is soft, but not brown.

5 Add the tomatoes, stock, tomato purée, thyme leaves, saffron threads and sugar, then bring to the boil, stirring to dissolve the tomato purée. Lower the heat, cover and simmer for 15 minutes. Adjust the seasoning.

6 Add the seafood and simmer until the clams open and the fish flakes easily. Discard the bouquet garni and any clams that do not open. Garnish with parsley and serve at once.

Salt Cod Fritters

Serves 6

INGREDIENTS

450 g/1 lb salt cod
350 g/12 oz floury baking
    potatoes
olive oil for frying
1 onion, very finely chopped

1 garlic clove, crushed
4 tbsp very finely chopped fresh
    parsley or coriander
1 tbsp capers in brine, drained
    and finely chopped (optional)

1 small egg, lightly beaten
salt and pepper
Aioli (see page 184), to serve
fresh flat-leaved parsley,
    to garnish

1 Break the salt cod into pieces and place in a bowl. Add enough water to cover and leave for 48 hours, changing the water 4 times.

2 Drain the salt cod, then cook in boiling water for 20–25 minutes until tender. Drain, then remove all the skin and bones. Using a fork, flake the fish into fine pieces that still retain some texture.

3 Meanwhile, boil the potatoes in their skins until tender. Drain, peel and mash in a large bowl. Set aside.

4 Heat 1 tablespoon oil in a frying pan. Add the onion and garlic and fry for 5 minutes, stirring, until tender but not brown. Remove with a slotted spoon and drain on kitchen paper.

5 Stir the salt cod, onion and garlic into the mashed potatoes. Stir in the parsley or coriander and capers, if using. Season generously with pepper.

6 Stir in the beaten egg. Cover and chill for 30 minutes, then adjust the seasoning.

7 Heat 5 cm/2 inches oil in a frying pan to 180–190°C/350–375°F, or until a cube of bread browns in 30 seconds. Drop tablespoonfuls of the salt-cod mixture into the hot oil and fry for about 8 minutes, or until golden brown and set. Do not fry more than 6 at a time because the oil will become too cold and the fritters will become soggy. You will get 18–20 fritters.

8 Drain the fritters on kitchen paper. Serve at once with aioli for dipping. Garnish with parsley.

Prawn Skewers with Tomato Salsa

Makes 8 skewers

INGREDIENTS

32 large tiger prawns
olive oil, for brushing
Skordalia (see page 188) or Aioli
    (see page 184), to serve

MARINADE
125 ml/4 fl oz extra-virgin
    olive oil
2 tbsp lemon juice

1 tsp finely chopped red chilli
1 tsp balsamic vinegar
pepper

TOMATO SALSA
2 large vine-ripened tomatoes
4 spring onions, white parts only,
    very finely chopped

1 red pepper, skinned, deseeded
    and chopped
1 orange or yellow pepper,
    skinned, deseeded and
    chopped
1 tbsp extra-virgin olive oil
2 tsp balsamic vinegar
4 sprigs fresh basil

1 To make the marinade, place all the ingredients in a non-metallic bowl and whisk together. Set aside.

2 To prepare the prawns, break off the heads. Peel off the shells, leaving the tails intact. Using a small knife, make a slit along the back and remove the thin black vein. Add the prawns to the marinade and stir until well coated. Cover and chill in the refrigerator for 15 minutes.

3 Make the salsa. Skin, core, deseed and chop the tomatoes. Put all the ingredients, except the basil, in a non-metallic bowl and toss together. Season to taste with salt and pepper.

4 Thread 4 prawns on to a metal skewer, bending each prawn in half. Repeat with 7 more skewers. Brush with marinade.

5 Brush a grill rack with oil. Place the skewers on the rack, then position under a preheated hot grill, about 7.5 cm/3 inches from the heat; cook for 1 minute. Turn them over, brush again and continue to cook for 1–1½ minutes until the prawns turn pink and opaque.

6 Tear the basil leaves and toss with the salsa. Arrange each skewer on a plate with some salsa and garnish with parsley. Serve with skordalia or aioli dip.

Swordfish à la Maltaise

Serves 4

INGREDIENTS

1 tbsp fennel seeds

2 tbsp fruity extra-virgin olive oil,
   plus extra for brushing
   and drizzling

2 large onions, thinly sliced

1 small garlic clove, crushed

4 swordfish steaks, about 175 g/
   6 oz each

1 large lemon, cut in half

2 large vine-ripened tomatoes,
   finely chopped

4 sprigs fresh thyme

salt and pepper

1 Place the fennel seeds in a dry frying pan over a medium-high heat and toast, stirring, until they give off their aroma, watching carefully that they do not burn. Immediately tip out of the pan on to a plate. Set this aside.

2 Heat 2 tablespoons of the olive oil in the pan. Add the onions and fry for 5 minutes, stirring occasionally. Add the garlic and continue frying the onions until very soft and tender, but not brown. Remove from the heat.

3 Cut out four 30 cm/ 12 inch circles of baking parchment. Very lightly brush the centre of each paper circle with olive oil. Equally divide the onions between the paper circles, flattening them out to about the size of the fish steaks.

4 Top the onions in each parcel with a swordfish steak. Squeeze lemon juice over the fish steaks and drizzle with a little olive oil. Scatter the tomatoes over the top, add a sprig of fresh thyme to each and season with salt and pepper to taste.

5 Fold the edges of the paper together, scrunching them tightly so no cooking juices escape during cooking. Place on a baking sheet and cook in a preheated oven at 200°C/400°F/Gas Mark 6 for 20 minutes.

6 To test if the fish is cooked, open one package and pierce the flesh with a knife – it should flake easily. Serve straight from the paper packages.

Mediterranean Monkfish

Serves 4

INGREDIENTS

600 g/1 lb 5 oz vine-ripened cherry tomatoes, a mixture of yellow and red, if available

2 monkfish fillets, about 350 g/12 oz each
8 tbsp Pesto Sauce (see page 124)

salt and pepper
fresh basil sprigs, to garnish
boiled new potatoes, to serve

1 Cut the tomatoes in half and scatter, cut-sides up, on the base of an ovenproof serving dish. Set aside.

2 Using your fingers, rub off the thin grey membrane that covers the monkfish.

3 If the skin has not been removed, place the fish skin-side down on a clean work surface. Loosen enough skin at one end of the fillet so you can grip hold of it. Work from the front of the fillet to the back. Insert the knife, almost flat, and using a gentle sawing action, remove the skin. Rinse the fillets

well and dry them with kitchen paper.

4 Place the fillets on top of the tomatoes, tucking the thin end under, if necessary (see Cook's Tip). Spread 4 tablespoons of the pesto sauce over each fillet and season with salt and pepper.

5 Cover the dish tightly with foil, shiny-side down. Place in a preheated oven at 230°C/450°F/Gas Mark 8 and roast for 16–18 minutes until the fish is cooked through, the flesh flakes easily and the tomatoes are dissolving into a thick sauce.

6 Adjust the seasoning, if necessary. Garnish with basil sprigs and serve at once with boiled new potatoes.

COOK'S TIP

Monkfish fillets are often cut from the tail, which means one end is much thinner than the rest and prone to over-cooking. If you can't get fillets that are the same thickness, fold the thin end under for even cooking.

Wrapped Red Mullet with Stewed Peppers & Fennel

Serves 4

INGREDIENTS

3 tbsp olive oil, plus extra for rubbing	2 large bulbs fennel, trimmed and thinly sliced	20–24 vine leaves in brine
	1 large clove garlic, crushed	1 lemon
2 large red peppers, cored, deseeded and thinly sliced	8 sprigs fresh thyme, plus extra for garnishing	4 red mullet, about 225 g/8 oz each, scaled and gutted
		salt and pepper

1 Heat the oil in a large frying pan over a medium–low heat. Add the peppers, fennel, garlic and 4 sprigs of thyme and stir together. Cook, stirring occasionally, for about 20 minutes until the vegetables are cooked thoroughly and are very soft, but not browned.

2 Meanwhile, rinse the vine leaves under cold, running water and pat dry with kitchen paper. Slice 4 thin slices off the lemon, then cut each slice in half. Finely grate the rind of half the lemon.

3 Stuff the mullet cavities with the lemon slices and remaining thyme sprigs. Rub a little olive oil on each fish and sprinkle with the lemon rind. Season with salt and pepper to taste.

4 Depending on the size of the mullet, wrap 5 or 6 vine leaves around each mullet, to enclose completely. Put the wrapped mullet on top of the fennel and peppers. Cover the pan and cook over a medium–low heat for 12–15 minutes until the fish are cooked through and the flesh flakes easily when tested with the tip of a knife.

5 Transfer the cooked fish to individual plates and spoon the fennel and peppers alongside. Garnish with thyme sprigs and serve.

Moules Marinières

Serves 4

INGREDIENTS

2 kg/4 lb 8 oz live mussels
4 tbsp olive oil
4–6 large garlic cloves, halved
800 g/1 lb 12 oz canned
    chopped tomatoes

300 ml/10 fl oz dry white wine
2 tbsp finely chopped fresh
    flat-leaved parsley, plus extra
    for garnishing

1 tbsp finely chopped fresh
    oregano
salt and pepper
French bread, to serve

1 Leave the mussels to soak in a bowl of lightly salted water for 30 minutes. Rinse them under cold running water and lightly scrub to remove any sand from the shells. Using a small, sharp knife, remove the 'beards' from the shells.

2 Discard any broken mussels or open mussels that do not shut when firmly tapped with the back of a knife. This indicates they are dead and could cause food poisoning if eaten. Rinse the mussels again, then set aside in a colander.

3 Heat the olive oil in a large saucepan or stockpot over a medium–high heat. Add the garlic and fry, stirring, for about 3 minutes to flavour the oil. Using a slotted spoon, remove the garlic from the pan.

4 Add the tomatoes and their juice, the wine, parsley and oregano and bring to the boil, stirring. Lower the heat, cover and simmer for 5 minutes to allow the flavours to blend.

5 Add the mussels, cover the pan and simmer for 5–8 minutes, shaking the pan regularly, until the mussels open. Using a slotted spoon, transfer the mussels to serving bowls, discarding any that are not open.

6 Season the sauce with salt and pepper to taste. Ladle the sauce over the mussels, sprinkle with extra chopped parsley and serve at once with plenty of French bread to mop up the delicious juices.

Seared Scallops with Champagne-Saffron Sauce

Serves 4

INGREDIENTS

generous pinch of saffron threads
about 60 g/2¼ oz unsalted butter
20 large scallops with the corals,
    each at least 2.5 cm/1 inch
    thick, shelled, juices reserved

4 tbsp dry champagne or
    sparkling wine
300 ml/10 fl oz double cream
½ lemon

salt and pepper
fresh flat-leaved parsley sprigs,
    to garnish

1 Heat a large, dry frying pan, preferably non-stick, over a high heat. Add the saffron threads and toast just until they start to give off their aroma. Immediately tip on to a plate and set aside.

2 Melt half the butter in the pan. Add half the scallops and fry for 2 minutes. Turn and fry for a further 1½–2 minutes until the scallops are set and the flesh is opaque all the way though when you pierce one with a knife (see Cook's Tip).

3 Transfer the scallops to a hot dish, cover and keep warm while cooking the rest in the same way, adding more butter as necessary.

4 Add the saffron to the cooking juices and pour in the champagne, cream and any reserved scallop juices, stirring. Bring to the boil, then lower the heat slightly and bubble for about 10 minutes until reduced to a consistency that coats the back of a spoon.

5 Add freshly squeezed lemon juice and salt and pepper to taste. Return the scallops to the pan and stir until just heated through. Transfer to 4 plates and garnish with parsley. Serve at once.

COOK'S TIP

If the scallops are thinner, only cook them for 1½ minutes on each side. Take great care not to overcook them.

Squid Salad

Serves 4–6

INGREDIENTS

900 g/2 lb small squid	4 vine-ripened tomatoes,	finely chopped red chillies
125 ml/4 fl oz lemon juice	deseeded and chopped	(optional)
50 ml/2 fl oz extra-virgin olive oil	salt and pepper	capers or black olives (optional)
25 g/1 oz fresh flat-leaved		fresh flat-leaved parsley,
parsley	TO GARNISH	finely chopped
8 spring onions	radicchio leaves	

1 To prepare each squid, pull the head and all the insides out of the body sac. Cut the tentacles off the head and discard the head. Remove the beak from the centre of the tentacles.

2 Pull out the thin, transparent quill that runs through the centre of the body. Rinse the body sac under running cold water and, using your fingers, rub off the thin, grey membrane. Cut the squid body sacs into 1 cm/½ inch slices. Rinse the tentacle pieces and set aside with the body slices.

3 Put the lemon juice and olive oil in a large bowl and stir together. Very finely chop the parsley and add to the bowl. Finely chop the white parts of the spring onions and add to the bowl with the tomatoes. Season with salt and pepper to taste.

4 Bring a pan of lightly salted water to the boil. Add all the squid and return to the boil.

5 As soon as the water returns to the boil, drain the squid. Add the squid to the bowl of dressing and

gently toss all the ingredients together.

6 Leave the squid to cool completely, then cover and leave to marinate in the refrigerator for at least 6 hours, preferably overnight.

7 Line a serving bowl with radicchio leaves. Add the chopped chilli, capers or olives, to taste, if using. Mound the squid salad on top of the radicchio leaves and sprinkle with finely chopped parsley. Serve thoroughly chilled.

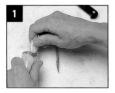

Salade Niçoise

Serves 4–6

INGREDIENTS

3 large eggs

250 g/9 oz French beans, topped and tailed

250 g/9 oz small waxy potatoes, such as Charlottes, scrubbed

1 large, sun-ripened tomato

1 large tuna steak, about 350 g/12 oz, and 2 cm/³⁄₄ inch thick, seared (see page 96)

60 g/2¼ oz Provençal-style Olives (see page 172), or plain black olives

50 g/1³⁄₄ oz canned anchovy fillets in oil, drained

1 tbsp chopped fresh flat-leaved parsley

GARLIC VINAIGRETTE

100 ml/3½ fl oz extra-virgin olive oil

3 tbsp red or white wine vinegar

½ tsp sugar

½ tsp Dijon mustard

2 garlic cloves, crushed

salt and pepper

1 To make the vinaigrette, put all the ingredients in a screw-top jar and shake until blended. Season with salt and pepper to taste. Set aside.

2 Bring 3 pans of water to the boil. Add the eggs to one pan, bring back to the boil, then cook for 12 minutes. Drain immediately and run under cold running water to stop further cooking.

3 Put the beans and potatoes (cut into halves) into

separate pans of boiling water. Blanch the beans for 3 minutes, then drain and immediately transfer to a large bowl. Shake the dressing and pour it over the beans.

4 Continue to cook the potatoes until they are tender, then drain and add to the beans and dressing while they are still hot. Leave the potatoes and beans to cool in the dressing.

5 Cut the tomato into eighths and add to the vegetables in the dressing. Toss together. Break the tuna into large chunks and gently toss with the other ingredients.

6 Shell the hard-boiled eggs and cut each into quarters lengthways.

7 Mound the tuna and vegetables on a large serving platter. Arrange the hard-boiled egg quarters around the side. Scatter the olives over the salad, then arrange the anchovies in a lattice on top. Cover and chill.

8 About 15 minutes before serving, remove the salad from the refrigerator. Spoon onto individual plates to serve.

Lobster Salad

Serves 2

INGREDIENTS

2 raw lobster tails	LEMON-DILL MAYONNAISE	TO GARNISH
	1 large lemon	radicchio leaves
	1 large egg yolk	lemon wedges
	½ tsp Dijon mustard	fresh dill sprigs
	150 ml/5 fl oz olive oil	
	1 tbsp chopped fresh dill	
	salt and pepper	

1 To make the lemon-dill mayonnaise, finely grate the rind from the lemon and squeeze the juice. Beat the egg yolk in a small bowl with the mustard and 1 teaspoon of the lemon juice.

2 Using a balloon whisk or electric mixer, beat in the olive oil, drop by drop, until a thick mayonnaise forms. Stir in half the lemon rind and 1 tablespoon of the juice.

3 Season with salt and pepper, and add more lemon juice, if desired. Stir in the dill and cover with cling film. Chill until required.

4 Bring a large saucepan of salted water to the boil. Add the lobster tails and continue to cook for 6 minutes until the flesh is opaque and the shells are red. Drain immediately and leave to cool completely.

5 Remove the lobster flesh from the shells and cut into bite-sized pieces.

6 Arrange the radicchio leaves on individual plates and top with the lobster flesh. Place a spoonful of the lemon-dill mayonnaise on the side. Garnish with lemon wedges and dill sprigs and serve.

Pasta with Broccoli & Anchovy Sauce

Serves 4

INGREDIENTS

500 g/1 lb 2 oz broccoli
400 g/14 oz dried orecchiette
    pasta
5 tbsp olive oil

2 large garlic cloves, crushed
50 g/1¾ oz canned anchovy
    fillets in oil, drained and
    finely chopped

60 g/2¼ oz Parmesan cheese
60 g/2¼ oz pecorino cheese
salt and pepper

1 Bring 2 pans of lightly salted water to the boil. Chop the broccoli florets and stems into small, bite-sized pieces. Add the broccoli to one pan and cook until very tender. Drain and set aside.

2 Put the pasta in the other pan of boiling water and cook for 10–12 minutes, or according to the instructions on the packet, until al dente.

3 Meanwhile, heat the olive oil in a large pan over a medium heat. Add the garlic and fry for 3 minutes, stirring, without allowing it to brown. Add the chopped anchovies to the oil and cook for 3 minutes, stirring and mashing with a wooden spoon to break them up. Finely grate the Parmesan and pecorino cheeses.

4 Drain the pasta, add to the pan of anchovies and stir. Add the broccoli and stir to mix.

5 Add the grated Parmesan and pecorino to the pasta and stir constantly over medium–high heat until the cheeses melt and the pasta and broccoli are coated.

6 Adjust the seasoning to taste – the anchovies and cheeses are salty, so you will only need to add pepper, if anything. Spoon into bowls or on to plates and serve at once.

VARIATION

Add dried chilli flakes to taste with the garlic in Step 3, if you want. If you have difficulty in finding orecchiette, try using pasta bows instead.

Linguine with Pesto Sauce

Serves 4; makes about 300 ml / 10 fl oz sauce

INGREDIENTS

400 g/14 oz dried or fresh
    linguine
freshly grated Parmesan cheese,
    to serve (optional)

PESTO SAUCE
150 g/5½ oz Parmesan cheese
3 garlic cloves, or to taste
150 g/5½ oz fresh basil leaves

5 tbsp pine kernels
150 ml/5 fl oz fruity extra-virgin
    olive oil
salt and pepper

1 To make the pesto sauce, cut the rind off the Parmesan and finely grate the cheese. Set aside. Cut each garlic clove in half lengthways and use the tip of the knife to lift out the green core, which can have a bitter flavour if the cloves are old. Coarsely chop the garlic.

2 Rinse the basil leaves and pat dry with kitchen paper. Put the basil in a food processor and add the pine kernels, grated cheese, chopped garlic and olive oil. Process for about 30 seconds, just until blended.

3 Add pepper and extra salt to taste, but remember the cheese is salty. Cover with a sheet of cling film and chill for up to 5 days.

4 Bring a large pan of water to the boil. Add ½ teaspoon salt and the linguine and cook according to the packet instructions until al dente. Drain well, reserving a few tablespoons of the cooking water.

5 Return the linguine to the pan over a low heat and stir in the sauce. Toss until the pasta is well coated and the sauce is heated

through. Stir in 2 tablespoons of the reserved cooking water if the sauce seems too thick. Serve at once with grated Parmesan for sprinkling over the top, if desired.

VARIATIONS

Use blanched almonds instead of pine kernels. To make a creamy dip to serve with sliced courgettes and pepper strips, stir 4 tablespoons of the pesto sauce into 4 tablespoons natural yogurt.

Spaghetti with Corsican Clam Sauce

Serves 4

INGREDIENTS

400 g/14 oz dried or fresh spaghetti	4 tbsp olive oil	60 g/2¼ oz Flavoured Olives (see page 172) of your choice, or plain green or black olives, stoned and chopped
salt and pepper	3 large garlic cloves, crushed	
	pinch of dried chilli flakes (optional)	
CORSICAN CLAM SAUCE	900 g/2 lb tomatoes, skinned and chopped, with juice reserved	1 tbsp chopped fresh oregano, or ½ tsp dried
900 g/2 lb clams in their shells		

1 Leave the clams to soak in a bowl of lightly salted water for 30 minutes. Rinse them under cold running water and lightly scrub to remove any sand from the shells.

2 Discard any broken clams or open clams that do not shut when firmly tapped with the back of a knife. This indicates they are dead and could cause food poisoning if eaten. Leave the clams to soak in a large bowl of water. Bring a large pan of lightly salted water to the boil for the pasta.

3 Heat the oil in a large frying pan over a medium heat. Add the garlic and chilli flakes, if using, and fry for about 2 minutes.

4 Stir in the tomatoes, olives and oregano. Lower the heat and simmer, stirring frequently, until the tomatoes soften and start to break up. Cover and simmer for 10 minutes.

5 Meanwhile, cook the spaghetti in the pan of boiling water according to the instructions on the packet until just al dente. Drain

well, reserving about 125 ml/ 4 fl oz of the cooking water. Keep the pasta warm.

6 Add the clams and reserved cooking liquid to the sauce and stir. Bring to the boil, stirring. Discard any clams that do not open; transfer to a larger pan.

7 Add the pasta to the sauce and toss until well coated. Transfer the pasta to individual dishes. Serve immediately.

Pasta with Tuna & Lemon

Serves 4

INGREDIENTS

60 g/2¼ oz butter, diced

300 ml/10 fl oz double cream

4 tbsp lemon juice

1 tbsp grated lemon rind

½ tsp anchovy essence

400 g/14 oz dried fusilli

200 g/7 oz canned tuna in olive
oil, drained and flaked

salt and pepper

TO GARNISH

2 tbsp finely chopped fresh
parsley

grated lemon zest

1 Bring a large saucepan of lightly salted water to the boil. Melt the butter in a large frying pan. Stir in the double cream and lemon juice and leave to simmer, stirring, for about 2 minutes until slightly thickened.

2 Stir in the lemon rind and anchovy essence. Meanwhile, cook the pasta for 10–12 minutes or according to the instructions on the packet until just al dente. Drain well.

3 Add the sauce to the pasta and toss until well coated. Add the tuna and gently toss until well blended but not too broken up.

4 Season to taste with salt and pepper. Transfer to a serving platter and garnish with the parsley and lemon zest. Grind over some pepper and serve at once.

COOK'S TIP

As an alternative, use the thin twist-shaped pasta casareccia instead.

VARIATION

For a vegetarian version, omit the tuna and anchovy essence. Add 150 g/5½ oz stoned olives instead. For extra 'kick' add a pinch of dried chilli flakes to the sauce instead of the anchovy essence.

Vegetables & Side Salads

The fresh produce from the Mediterranean is some of the most luscious and flavourful in the world. Slowly ripened under the hot Mediterranean sun, aubergines, courgettes, peppers and tomatoes look so fantastic you can almost taste them with your eyes.

With such full flavours, you'll find the vegetable dishes are not complicated. For a Mediterranean touch, serve globe artichokes with a classic Hollandaise sauce flavoured with blood-orange juice. Or, for another simple recipe, savour Broad Beans with Feta & Lemon – it's delicious served hot or cold. Char-grilled Vegetable Platter makes the most of fresh produce at its peak, while slow-cook stews, such as the classic Ratatouille, enhance the flavours of vegetables which are starting to pass their prime.

Salads feature prominently in Mediterranean meals, and there can't be many dishes more typically Mediterranean than Roasted Pepper Salad or Mozzarella & Cherry Tomato Salad. Both have simple dressings and they make ideal accompaniments or first courses. And, at any time of the year, it's difficult to beat Panzanella, the Italian salad based on leftover bread and made into a colourful medley with refreshing tomatoes, cucumbers and peppers.

Char-grilled Vegetable Platter

Serves 4–6

INGREDIENTS

2 kg/4 lb 8 oz mixed fresh
    vegetables, such as chicory,
    aubergines, courgettes, fennel,

peppers, spring onions
garlic-flavoured olive oil
salt and pepper

fresh basil leaves, to garnish

1 Prepare the vegetables as necessary. Top and tail the aubergines and cut into 5 mm/¼ inch slices. Cut each head of chicory in half lengthways.

2 Top and tail the courgettes and cut into 5 mm/¼ inch slices. Remove the fronds from the fennel and slice thickly across the grain.

3 Cut the peppers into quarters, then remove the cores and seeds. Trim the top green part of the spring onions, and cut in half lengthways if large.

4 As each vegetable is prepared, put it in a large bowl, drizzle with the garlic oil and season lightly with salt and pepper. Using your hands, toss the vegetables together so they are lightly coated with oil; the vegetables should not be dripping in oil.

5 Heat a large, ridged cast-iron frying pan over a high heat. Lightly brush with oil. Add a batch of vegetables – enough to fit in the pan in a single layer. Cook the vegetables on one side over medium–high heat until they are starting to turn limp.

6 Brush the half-cooked vegetables with a little more oil, then turn them. Continue cooking until they are tender – the exact cooking times will depend on the age and thickness of the vegetables. Transfer to a large platter and repeat with the remaining vegetables.

7 While still hot, sprinkle the vegetables with salt and pepper. Garnish with basil leaves and serve.

Ratatouille

Serves 4

INGREDIENTS

1 large aubergine, about 300 g/10½ oz	800 g/1 lb 12 oz canned chopped tomatoes	and 1 bay leaf, tied in a 7.5 cm/3 inch piece of celery
5 tbsp olive oil	1 tsp sugar	salt and pepper
2 large onions, thinly sliced	1 bouquet garni of 2 sprigs fresh	fresh basil leaves, to garnish
2 large garlic cloves, crushed	thyme, 2 large sprigs fresh	
4 courgettes, sliced	parsley, 1 sprig fresh basil	

1 Coarsely chop the aubergine, then place in a colander. Sprinkle with salt and leave for 30 minutes to drain. Rinse well and pat dry.

2 Heat the oil in a large, heavy-based flameproof casserole over a medium heat. Add the onions, lower the heat and fry, stirring frequently, for 10 minutes.

3 Add the garlic and continue to fry for 2 minutes until the onions are very tender, and just lightly browned.

4 Add the aubergine, courgettes, tomatoes and their juice, the sugar, bouquet garni and salt and pepper to taste. Bring to the boil, then lower the heat to very low, cover and leave for 30 minutes.

5 Adjust the seasoning. Remove and discard the bouquet garni. Garnish the vegetable stew with basil leaves and serve.

COOK'S TIP

This is equally good served hot, at room temperature or chilled. To make a vegetarian meal, serve it over cooked couscous (see page 80), or with Green Tabbouleh (see page 166).

Artichokes with Sauce Maltaise

Serves 4

INGREDIENTS

4 large globe artichokes	SAUCE MALTAISE	3 tbsp water
2 lemon slices	1 blood orange	3 egg yolks
	175 g/6 oz butter	salt and pepper
	2–3 tbsp lemon juice	

1 To prepare the globe artichokes, bring lightly salted water to the boil in a pan large enough to hold the 4 artichokes upright. Add the lemon slices. Break off the stems and trim the bases of the artichokes so they are flat and will sit upright on a plate.

2 Put the artichokes in the pan and place a heatproof plate on top. Lower the heat and simmer for 20–25 minutes, until you can easily pull out a leaf.

3 Meanwhile, make the sauce. Finely grate the rind from the orange and squeeze 2 tablespoons orange juice. Put the butter in a saucepan over medium heat and melt, skimming the surface.

4 Put 2 tablespoons of the lemon juice, the water, plus salt and pepper, in a bowl. Set it over a pan of simmering water, making sure the base of the bowl does not come into contact with the water. Whisk until heated.

5 Whisk in the egg yolks, until blended and warmed through. Add the hot butter in a steady stream, whisking constantly until a thick, smooth sauce forms.

6 Stir in the orange rind and juice. Adjust the seasoning, adding extra lemon juice if necessary. Remove from the heat.

7 Drain the artichokes. Place each on a plate with a ramekin of the Sauce Maltaise.

COOK'S TIP

Pull out the leaves, starting with the outer layer, until you get to the thin purple leaves, which are inedible. Dip the bottom of each leaf into the sauce and scrape off the fleshy part with your teeth. Cut off the central core of leaves and the hairy choke to reveal the delicious bottom, that can be cut with a knife and fork.

Baked Aubergine Gratin

Serves 4–6

INGREDIENTS

1 large aubergine, about 800 g/1 lb 12 oz	85 g/3 oz Parmesan cheese	or good-quality bottled tomato sauce for pasta
salt	olive oil	salt and pepper
300 g/10½ oz mozzarella cheese	250 ml/9 fl oz Slow-cooked Tomato Sauce (see page 192),	

1 Top and tail the aubergine and, using a sharp knife, cut into 5 mm/¼ inch slices crossways. Arrange the slices on a large plate, sprinkle with salt and set aside for 30 minutes to drain.

2 Meanwhile, drain and grate the mozzarella cheese and finely grate the Parmesan cheese. Set aside.

3 Rinse the aubergine slices and pat dry with kitchen paper. Lightly brush a baking sheet with olive oil and arrange the aubergine slices in a single layer. Brush the tops with olive oil.

4 Roast in a preheated oven at 200°C/400°F/Gas Mark 6 for 5 minutes. Using tongs, turn the slices, then brush with a little more oil and bake for a further 5 minutes, or until the aubergine is just cooked through and tender. Do not turn off the oven.

5 Pour out and spread about 1 tablespoon olive oil over the bottom of a gratin dish or other ovenproof serving dish.

Add a layer of aubergine slices, about a quarter of the tomato sauce, and top with a quarter of the mozzarella. Season to taste with salt and pepper.

6 Continue layering until all the ingredients are used, ending with a layer of sauce. Sprinkle the Parmesan cheese over the top. Bake in the oven for 30 minutes until bubbling. Leave to stand for 5 minutes before serving.

Imam Bayildi

Serves 4

INGREDIENTS

2 aubergines, about
    300 g/10½ oz each
5 tbsp olive oil
2 large onions, finely chopped
2 large garlic cloves, crushed
800 g/1 lb 12 oz canned
    chopped tomatoes

3 tbsp raisins
3 tbsp finely chopped fresh
    flat-leaved parsley
finely grated rind of ½ unwaxed
    lemon
2 tbsp lemon juice
½ tsp ground cinnamon

½ tsp ground cumin
pinch of cayenne pepper
salt and pepper
fresh flat-leaved parsley sprigs,
    to garnish

1 Cut each aubergine in half lengthways. Using a knife, scoop out the flesh from each half, leaving a 5 mm/¼ inch shell all around. Set the shells aside.

2 Finely chop the aubergine flesh, place in a colander, sprinkle with salt and leave for 30 minutes to drain. Rinse and pat dry.

3 Heat 3 tablespoons of the olive oil in a large frying pan. Add the onions and fry, stirring frequently, over a medium–high heat until they are softened. Add the garlic and continue frying for 2 minutes, stirring.

4 Add the tomatoes, aubergine flesh, raisins, parsley, lemon rind, lemon juice, cinnamon, cumin and cayenne pepper, then season with salt and pepper to taste. Simmer for 20 minutes, stirring occasionally, until the mixture has thickened.

5 Spoon the mixture into the aubergine shells, mounding it up slightly. Place the filled shells in an ovenproof dish and add the remaining olive oil.

6 Cover the dish with foil. Roast in a preheated oven at 180°C/350°F/ Gas Mark 4 for 45–50 minutes until the aubergine shells are tender and the filling is hot. Serve hot, or leave to cool, then chill until required. Garnish with sprigs of parsley.

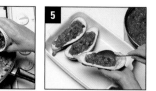

Sweet & Sour Courgettes

Serves 4-6

INGREDIENTS

500 g/1 lb 2 oz courgettes
3 tbsp olive oil
1 large garlic clove, finely
    chopped
3 tbsp red or white wine vinegar

3 tbsp water
6-8 anchovy fillets, canned
    or salted
3 tbsp pine kernels
30 g/1¼ oz raisins

salt and pepper
fresh flat-leaved parsley sprigs,
    to garnish

1 Top and tail the courgettes, then use a sharp knife to cut them into long, thin strips. Heat the oil in a large frying pan over a medium heat. Add the garlic and fry, stirring, for about 2 minutes.

2 Add the courgettes and cook, stirring, until they just start to turn brown. Add the wine vinegar and water, cover and simmer for 10 minutes, stirring.

3 Meanwhile, drain the anchovies if canned, or rinse if they are salted. Coarsely chop, then use the back of a wooden spoon to mash them to a paste.

4 Stir the anchovies, pine kernels and raisins into the pan. Increase the heat and stir until the courgettes are coated in a thin sauce and are tender. Adjust the seasoning, remembering that the anchovies are very salty.

5 Either serve at once, or leave the courgettes to cool completely and serve at room temperature. To serve, garnish with fresh parsley sprigs.

VARIATION

Replace the raisins with sultanas. Add a little grated lemon or orange rind for added zing.

Deep-fried Courgettes

Serves 4

INGREDIENTS

5 tbsp cornflour
1 tsp salt
pinch of cayenne pepper, or
    to taste

150 ml/5 fl oz water
900 g/2 lb courgettes
vegetable oil, for frying
sea salt, to serve

fresh herb sprigs, such as basil,
    flat-leaved parsley or sage,
    to garnish

1 Sift the cornflour, salt and cayenne pepper into a large mixing bowl and make a well in the centre. Pour in the water and beat until just blended to make a thin batter. The batter may have a few lumps but this does not matter. Set aside for 20 minutes.

2 Meanwhile, cut the courgettes into 5 mm/ ¼ inch slices. Heat the oil in a deep frying pan or deep-fat fryer to 190°C/375°F or until a cube of bread sizzles in 20 seconds.

3 Stir the batter. Working in batches, put some courgette slices in the batter and stir around until coated. Using a slotted spoon, remove the slices from the batter, shaking off the excess.

4 Drop the coated courgette slices into the hot oil and fry for about 45–60 seconds, or until just golden brown on each side. Immediately remove from the oil and drain well on crumpled kitchen paper. Sprinkle with sea salt and keep warm if not serving straight away.

5 Repeat this process with the remaining courgette slices. You can serve them garnished with a variety of herbs, according to what is available.

COOK'S TIP

It is important to get the oil to the correct temperature, otherwise the fried courgettes will be soggy.

VARIATION

Fry red onion rings coated with the batter.

Braised Fennel

Serves 4–6

INGREDIENTS

2 lemon slices

2–3 bulbs fennel, depending
   on size

1½ tbsp olive oil

40 g/1½ oz butter

4 sprigs fresh thyme, or
   ½ tbsp dried

175 ml/6 fl oz chicken or
   vegetable stock

85 g/3 oz freshly grated
   Parmesan cheese

pepper

extra thyme, to garnish

1 Bring a large saucepan of
water to the boil and add
the lemon slices. Trim the
fennel bulbs and slice each
one lengthways. Put them in
the boiling water, bring back
to the boil and simmer for
about 8 minutes until almost
tender. Drain well.

2 Put the olive oil and
butter in a flameproof
casserole and melt over
medium heat. Swirl the
melted mixture around so
the bottom and sides of the
casserole are well coated.

3 Add the fennel slices and
stir until coated. Add the
thyme and pepper to taste.
Pour in the stock. Sprinkle
the cheese over the top.

4 Bake in a preheated oven
at 200°C/400°F/Gas
Mark 6 for 25–30 minutes
until the fennel has absorbed
the stock and is tender, and
the cheese has melted and
become golden brown.
Garnish with thyme sprigs
and serve at once.

COOK'S TIP

*This is an ideal way to
serve older fennel bulbs.*

Mixed Vegetables à la Grecque

Serves 4–6

INGREDIENTS

250 g/9 oz small pickling onions
250 g/9 oz mushrooms
250 g/9 oz courgettes
450 ml/16 fl oz water
5 tbsp olive oil
2 tbsp lemon juice
2 strips lemon rind

2 large garlic cloves, thinly sliced
½ Spanish onion, finely chopped
1 bay leaf
15 black peppercorns, lightly
    crushed
10 coriander seeds, lightly
    crushed

pinch of dried oregano
finely chopped fresh flat-leaved
    parsley or coriander,
    to garnish
focaccia, to serve

1 Put a kettle of water on to boil. Put the small onions in a heatproof bowl and pour over boiling water to cover. Leave to stand for 2 minutes, then drain well. Using a small knife and your fingers, peel off the skins, which should slip off easily.

2 Trim the mushroom stems; cut the mushrooms into halves or quarters if they are large, or leave whole. Top and tail the courgettes, cut off strips of the peel for a decorative finish, then cut into 5 mm/ ¼ inch slices. Set both aside.

3 Put the water, olive oil, lemon juice and rind, garlic, Spanish onion, bay leaf, peppercorns, coriander seeds and oregano in a saucepan over a high heat and bring to the boil. Lower the heat and simmer for 15 minutes.

4 Add the small onions and continue to simmer for 5 minutes. Add the courgettes and mushrooms, and simmer for a further 2 minutes. Using a slotted spoon, transfer all the vegetables to a heatproof dish.

5 Turn up the heat to return the liquid to the boil, and boil until reduced to about 6 tablespoons. Pour over the vegetables and set aside to cool completely.

6 Cover the dish with cling film and chill for at least 12 hours.

7 To serve, put the vegetables and cooking liquid in a serving dish and scatter the fresh herbs over. Serve with chunks of focaccia bread.

Glazed Baby Onions

Serves 4–6

INGREDIENTS

500 g/1 lb 2 oz baby onions
2 tbsp olive oil
2 large garlic cloves, crushed

300 ml/10 fl oz vegetable or
    chicken stock
1 tbsp fresh thyme leaves
1 tbsp light brown sugar
2 tbsp red wine vinegar

about ½ tbsp best-quality
    balsamic vinegar
salt and pepper
fresh thyme sprigs, to garnish

1 Bring a kettle of water to the boil. Put the onions in a large, heatproof bowl, pour over enough boiling water to cover and leave to stand for 2 minutes. Drain well.

2 Using a small knife and your fingers, peel off the skins, which should slip off easily.

3 Heat the olive oil in a large frying pan over a medium-high heat. Add the onions and stir for about 8 minutes, until they are golden on all sides.

4 Add the garlic and cook for 2 minutes, stirring. Add the stock, thyme leaves, sugar and red wine vinegar, stirring until the sugar has completely dissolved.

5 Bring to the boil, then lower the heat and simmer for 10 minutes, or until the onions are tender when you pierce them with the tip of a knife and the cooking liquid is reduced to a syrupy glaze.

6 Stir in ½ tablespoon balsamic vinegar. Season to taste with salt and pepper and extra balsamic vinegar, if desired. Transfer to a serving dish and serve hot or cold, garnished with several fresh thyme sprigs.

VARIATION

For extra texture, stir in 2 tablespoons toasted pine kernels just before serving. Do not add them earlier or they will become soft.

Spiced Lentils with Spinach

Serves 4–6

INGREDIENTS

2 tbsp olive oil
1 large onion, finely chopped
1 large garlic clove, crushed
½ tbsp ground cumin
½ tsp ground ginger
250 g/9 oz Puy lentils

about 600 ml/1 pint vegetable or
    chicken stock
100 g/3½ oz baby spinach leaves
2 tbsp fresh mint leaves

1 tbsp fresh coriander leaves
1 tbsp fresh flat-leaved
    parsley leaves
freshly squeezed lemon juice
salt and pepper
grated lemon zest, to garnish

1 Heat the olive oil in a large frying pan over a medium-high heat. Add the onion and cook for about 6 minutes. Stir in the garlic, cumin and ginger and continue cooking, stirring occasionally, until the onion just starts to brown.

2 Stir in the lentils. Pour in enough stock to cover the lentils by 2.5 cm/1 inch and bring to the boil. Lower the heat and simmer for 20 minutes, or according to the packet instructions, until the lentils are tender.

3 Meanwhile, rinse the spinach leaves in several changes of cold water and shake dry. Finely chop the mint, coriander and parsley leaves.

4 If there isn't any stock left in the pan, add a little extra. Add the spinach and stir through until it just wilts. Stir in the mint, coriander and parsley. Adjust the seasoning, adding lemon juice and salt and pepper. Transfer to a serving bowl and serve, garnished with lemon zest.

COOK'S TIP

This recipe uses green lentils from Puy in France because they are good at keeping their shape even after long cooking. You can, however, also use orange or brown lentils but it is necessary to watch them while they cook or they will quickly turn to a mush.

Borlotti Beans in Tomato Sauce

Serves 4–6

INGREDIENTS

600 g/1 lb 5 oz fresh borlotti
    beans, in shells
4 large leaves fresh sage, torn
1 tbsp olive oil
1 large onion, finely sliced

300 ml/10 fl oz Slow-cooked
    Tomato Sauce (see page 192),
    or good-quality bottled
    tomato sauce for pasta
salt and pepper

extra shredded fresh sage leaves
    (chopped), to garnish

1 Shell the borlotti beans. Bring a saucepan of water to the boil, add the beans and torn sage leaves and simmer for about 12 minutes, or until tender. Drain and set aside.

2 Heat the oil in a large frying pan over a medium heat. Add the onion and cook, stirring occasionally, for about 5 minutes until soft but not brown. Stir the tomato sauce into the pan with the cooked borlotti beans and the torn sage leaves.

3 Increase the heat and bring to the boil, stirring. Lower the heat, partially cover and simmer for about 10 minutes, or until the sauce has slightly reduced.

4 Adjust the seasoning, transfer to a serving bowl and serve hot, garnished with fresh sage leaves.

VARIATION

If fresh borlotti beans are unavailable, use canned instead. Drain and rinse, then add with the sage and tomato sauce in Step 2.

Broad Beans with Feta & Lemon

Serves 4–6

INGREDIENTS

500 g/1 lb 2 oz shelled
   broad beans
4 tbsp extra-virgin olive oil
1 tbsp lemon juice

1 tbsp finely chopped fresh dill,
   plus a little extra for
   garnishing

60 g/2¼ oz feta cheese, drained
   and diced
salt and pepper
lemon wedges, to serve

1 Bring a saucepan of water to the boil. Add the broad beans and cook for about 2 minutes until tender. Drain well.

2 When the beans are cool enough to handle, remove and discard the outer skins, to reveal the bright green beans underneath (see Cook's Tip). Put the peeled beans in a serving bowl.

3 Stir together the olive oil and lemon juice, then season with salt and pepper to taste. Pour over the warm beans, add the dill and stir together. Adjust the seasoning, if necessary.

4 If serving hot, toss with the feta cheese and sprinkle with extra dill. Alternatively, leave to cool and chill until required. Remove from the refrigerator 10 minutes before serving, season, then sprinkle with the feta and extra dill. Serve with lemon wedges.

COOK'S TIP

It's worth using a good-quality olive oil, because it will make all the difference to the flavour of the finished dish.

COOK'S TIP

If you are lucky enough to have very young broad beans at the start of the season, it isn't necessary to remove the outer skin.

Mozzarella & Cherry Tomato Salad

Serves 4-6

INGREDIENTS

450 g/1 lb cherry tomatoes
4 spring onions
125 ml/4 fl oz extra-virgin
   olive oil

2 tbsp best-quality balsamic
   vinegar
200 g/7 oz buffalo mozzarella,
   cut into cubes

15 g/¹⁄₂ oz fresh flat-leaved
   parsley
25 g/1 oz fresh basil leaves
salt and pepper

1 Using a sharp knife, cut the tomatoes in half and put in a large bowl. Trim the spring onions and finely chop the green and white parts, then add to the bowl.

2 Pour in the olive oil and balsamic vinegar and use your hands to toss together. Season with salt and pepper, add the mozzarella and toss again. Cover and chill in the refrigerator for 4 hours.

3 Remove from the refrigerator 10 minutes before serving. Finely chop the parsley and add to the salad. Toss all the ingredients together again. Tear the basil leaves over the salad. Adjust the seasoning and serve.

COOK'S TIP

For the best flavour, buy buffalo mozzarella – mozzarella di bufala – rather than the factory-made cow's milk version. This salad would also look good made with bocconcini which are small balls of mozzarella. Look out for these in Italian delicatessens.

VARIATIONS

Replace the cherry tomatoes with Oven-dried Tomatoes (see page 174), or drained sun-dried tomatoes soaked in oil.

To make this salad more substantial, stir in 400 g/ 14 oz cooked and cooled pasta shapes. When the pasta is al dente, drain well and toss with 1 tablespoon olive oil and leave to cool completely before adding to the tomatoes and mozzarella in Step 2.

Roasted Pepper Salad

Serves 4

INGREDIENTS

4–6 large red, yellow and/or
  orange peppers
2 spring onions, trimmed

LEMON-PARSLEY VINAIGRETTE
6 tbsp extra-virgin olive oil
1½ tbsp freshly squeezed
  lemon juice

2 tbsp finely chopped fresh flat-
  leaved parsley
salt and pepper

1 To make the dressing, put the oil, lemon juice and parsley in a screw-top jar and shake until well blended. Add salt and pepper to taste. Set aside.

2 Slice the tops off the peppers, then cut each into quarters or thirds, depending on the size. Remove the cores and seeds – the flatter the pieces are, the easier they are to cook.

3 Finely slice the spring onions crosswise.

4 Place the pepper pieces on a grill rack under a preheated hot grill and grill for about 10 minutes, or until the skins are charred and the flesh is softened.

5 Using tongs, remove each piece as it is ready. Immediately place in a bowl and cover with cling film. Set aside for 20 minutes to allow the steam to loosen the skins.

6 When cool, carefully use a small, sharp knife or your fingers to remove all of the skins from the peppers, then slice the pepper flesh into long, thin strips.

7 Arrange the pepper strips on a serving platter. Shake the dressing again, then pour over the salad. Scatter the spring onions over the top. Serve at once with crusty bread, or cover and chill until required.

VARIATION

For a party, marinate small cooked prawns in the dressing and scatter them over the salad. Other ingredients you can add to the salad include capers, anchovies, pitted and sliced green or black olives, and finely grated lemon rind.

Stuffed Tomato Salad

Makes 4

INGREDIENTS

about 40 g/1½ oz cucumber, finely diced	5 spring onions, trimmed and sliced	squeeze of lemon juice
3 large eggs	350 g/12 oz canned tuna in olive oil, drained	small handful of fresh basil leaves, plus extra for garnishing
4 extra-large tomatoes, about 300 g/10½ oz each	1–2 tbsp mayonnaise	salt and pepper

1 Put the cucumber in a nylon sieve, sprinkle with salt and leave to drain for 30 minutes.

2 Meanwhile, bring a pan of water to the boil, add the eggs and cook for 12 minutes. Drain and place under running cold water to stop the cooking process.

3 Shell the eggs and chop the yolks and whites separately. Rinse the cucumber thoroughly and pat dry with kitchen paper.

4 Working with one tomato at a time, slice off the top and use a small spoon to scoop out the insides; reserve the insides. Drain the tomatoes upside-down on kitchen paper. Chop the reserved scooped-out insides and drain.

5 Put the chopped tomato in a bowl and add the chopped cucumber, sliced spring onions, all the egg yolks and most of the egg white, reserving a little to sprinkle over the tops. Flake in the tuna.

6 Add 1 tablespoon of the mayonnaise, the lemon juice and salt and pepper to taste. Stir together and add a little more mayonnaise if the mixture is too thick. Tear the basil leaves and stir into the mixture. Adjust the seasoning, if necessary.

7 Spoon the filling into the hollowed-out tomatoes. Sprinkle the tops with the reserved egg white. Cover with cling film and chill until required, but not for more than 3 hours or the filling will become soggy. Garnish with basil leaves and serve.

Panzanella

Serves 4

INGREDIENTS

250 g/9 oz stale Herb Foccacia (see page 206) or ciabatta bread or French bread

4 large, vine-ripened tomatoes

4 red, yellow and/or orange peppers

about 5 tbsp extra-virgin olive oil

100 g/3½ oz cucumber

1 large red onion, finely chopped

8 canned anchovy fillets, drained and chopped

2 tbsp capers in brine, rinsed and patted dry

about 4 tbsp red wine vinegar

about 2 tbsp best-quality balsamic vinegar

salt and pepper

fresh basil leaves, to garnish

1 Cut the bread into 2.5 cm/1 inch cubes and place in a large bowl. Working over a plate to catch any juices, quarter the tomatoes; reserve the juices. Using a teaspoon, scoop out the cores and seeds, then finely chop the flesh. Add to the bread cubes.

2 Drizzle 5 tablespoons of olive oil over the mixture and toss with your hands until well coated. Pour in the reserved tomato juice and toss again. Cover and set aside for about 30 minutes.

3 Meanwhile, cut the peppers in half and remove the cores and seeds. Place on a grill rack under a preheated hot grill and grill for 10 minutes, or until the skins are charred and the flesh softened. Place in a plastic bag, seal and set aside for 20 minutes to allow the steam to loosen the skins. Remove the skins, then finely chop the peppers.

4 Cut the cucumber in half lengthways, then cut each half into 3 strips lengthways. Using a teaspoon, scoop out and discard the seeds. Dice the cucumber.

5 Add the onion, peppers, cucumber, anchovy fillets and capers to the bread and toss together. Sprinkle with the red wine and balsamic vinegars and season to taste with salt and pepper. Drizzle with extra olive oil or vinegar if necessary, but be cautious that it does not become too greasy or soggy. Sprinkle the fresh basil leaves over the salad and serve at once.

Green Tabbouleh

Serves 4

INGREDIENTS

300 g/10½ oz bulgar wheat	15 g/½ oz fresh flat-leaved	about 2 tbsp garlic-flavoured
200 g/7 oz cucumber	parsley	olive oil
6 spring onions	1 unwaxed lemon	salt and pepper

1 Bring a kettle of water to the boil. Place the bulgar wheat in a heatproof bowl, pour over 600 ml/1 pint boiling water and cover with an upturned plate. Set aside for at least 20 minutes until the wheat absorbs the water and becomes tender.

2 While the wheat is soaking, cut the cucumber in half lengthways and then cut each half into 3 strips lengthways. Using a teaspoon, scoop out and discard the seeds. Chop the cucumber strips into bite-sized pieces. Put the cucumber pieces in a serving bowl.

3 Trim the top of the green parts of each of the spring onions, then cut each in half lengthways. Finely chop and add to the cucumber in the bowl.

4 Place the parsley on a chopping board and sprinkle with salt. Using a cook's knife, very finely chop both the leaves and stems. Add to the bowl with the cucumber and onions. Finely grate the lemon rind into the bowl.

5 When the bulgar wheat is cool enough to handle, either squeeze out any excess water with your hands or press out the water through a sieve, then add to the bowl with the other ingredients.

6 Cut the lemon in half and squeeze the juice of one half over the salad. Add 2 tablespoons of the garlic-flavoured oil and stir all the ingredients together. Adjust the seasoning with salt and pepper to taste and extra lemon juice or oil if needed. Cover with cling film and chill until required.

COOK'S TIP

Serve as a meze with dips such as Hummus (see page 8).

Radicchio & Lardon Salad

Serves 4

INGREDIENTS

600 g/1 lb 5 oz radicchio, 3 or 4
    heads, depending on size
about 3 tbsp olive oil

1 large garlic clove, crushed
300 g/10½ oz lardons
about 1 tbsp best-quality
    balsamic vinegar

salt and pepper
fresh basil leaves, to garnish

1 Remove enough of the outer leaves from the radicchio heads to line 4 individual plates. Cut the remaining radicchio into 5 mm/¼ inch slices (across the grain).

2 Heat 3 tablespoons of oil in a large frying pan over a medium-high heat. Add the garlic clove and fry, stirring, for 2 minutes. Remove from the pan with a slotted spoon.

3 Add the lardons and fry for about 5 minutes, or until they are cooked through and brown on the outside: do not overcook.

4 Add the radicchio to the pan and toss for about 30 seconds, just until it is heated through and starting to become limp but do not leave it long enough to become soggy (see Cook's Tip).

5 Add 1 tablespoon of the balsamic vinegar and toss again. Drizzle with extra oil or vinegar, if desired. Add salt and pepper to taste. Spoon the hot salad on to the radicchio-lined plates and garnish with fresh basil leaves. Serve at once.

COOK'S TIP

It is important not to overcook the radicchio in Step 4 or it will become grey. Just warm it through.

Accompaniments

You'll find a collection of diverse recipes in this chapter. These are the recipes that help you add a Mediterranean flavour to any meal you serve. Use the Mediterranean Fish Stock, for example, when you want to make a soup with subtle, authentic flavouring, or make Flavoured Olives, preserved in olive oil, to have to hand when friends stop by for a drink.

Wherever you live, the chances are that there will be a glut of tomatoes at some time. Try the Mediterranean trick of slow-roasting the tomatoes, then storing them in olive oil so you can add their fresh flavour to pasta sauces and casseroles throughout the year. Or you can make large batches of Slow-cooked Tomato Sauce and stock the freezer.

The breads in this chapter are flavoured with some of the region's most distinctive flavourings – Herb Focaccia makes a good accompaniment to any meal; Olive Rolls have so much flavour they can be munched on their own or made into delicious sandwiches; and Sesame Breadsticks, soft on the inside with a crisp exterior, disappear in a flash when served with one of the creamy dips.

Greeks, Cypriots and Turks, in particular, enjoy thick, creamy yogurt with just about every meal of the day. In some parts of the world this is readily available in supermarkets, but if you can't get it, follow the recipe in this chapter for Greek Strained Yogurt.

Flavoured Olives

Each fills a 500 ml / 18 fl oz preserving jar

INGREDIENTS

fresh herb sprigs, such as
coriander, flat-leaved parsley
or thyme, to serve

PROVENCAL-STYLE OLIVES

3 dried red chillies
1 tsp black peppercorns
300 g/10½ oz black Niçoise olives
in brine
2 lemon slices
1 tsp black mustard seeds
1 tbsp garlic-flavoured olive oil
fruity extra-virgin olive oil

CATALAN-STYLE OLIVES

½ grilled red or orange pepper
(see page 164)
150 g/5½ oz black olives in brine
150 g/5½ oz green pimento-
stuffed olives in brine
1 tbsp capers in brine, rinsed
pinch of dried chilli flakes, or
to taste
4 tbsp coarsely chopped fresh
coriander leaves
1 bay leaf
fruity extra-virgin olive oil

CRACKED GREEK-STYLE OLIVES

½ large lemon
300 g/10½ oz kalamata olives
in brine
4 sprigs fresh thyme
1 shallot, very finely chopped
1 tbsp fennel seeds, lightly
crushed
1 tsp dried dill
fruity extra-virgin olive oil

1 To make the Provençal-style olives, place the dried red chillies and black peppercorns in a mortar and lightly crush. Drain and rinse the olives, then pat dry with kitchen paper. Put all the ingredients in a 500 ml/18 fl oz preserving jar, pouring over enough olive oil to cover the olives.

2 Seal the jar and leave for at least 10 days before serving, shaking the jar daily.

3 To make the Catalan-style olives, finely chop the pepper. Drain and rinse both olives, then pat dry with kitchen paper. Put all the ingredients into a 500 ml/18 fl oz preserving jar, pouring over enough olive

oil to cover. Seal and marinate as in Step 2.

4 To make the cracked Greek-style olives, cut the lemon into 4 slices, then cut each slice into wedges. Drain and rinse the olives, then pat them dry with kitchen paper.

5 Slice each olive lengthways on one side down to the stone. Put all the ingredients in a 500 ml/18 fl oz preserving jar, pouring over olive oil to cover. Seal and marinate as in Step 2.

Oven-dried Tomatoes

Makes enough to fill a 250 ml / 9 fl oz preserving jar

INGREDIENTS

1 kg/2 lb 4 oz large, juicy
   full-flavoured tomatoes

sea salt
extra-virgin olive oil

1 Using a sharp knife, cut each of the tomatoes into quarters lengthways.

2 Using a teaspoon, scoop out the seeds and discard. If the tomatoes are large, cut each quarter in half lengthways again.

3 Sprinkle sea salt in a roasting tin and arrange the tomato slices, skin-side down, on top. Roast in a preheated oven at 120°C/250°F/Gas Mark ½ for 2½ hours, or until the edges are just starting to look charred and the flesh is dry but still pliable. The exact roasting time and yield will depend on the size and

juiciness of the tomatoes. Check the tomatoes at 30 minute intervals after 1½ hours.

4 Remove the dried tomatoes from the pan and leave to cool completely. Put into a 250 ml/9 fl oz preserving jar and pour over enough olive oil to cover. Seal the jar tightly and store in the refrigerator, where it will keep for up to 2 weeks.

COOK'S TIP

Serve these oven-dried tomatoes with slices of buffalo mozzarella: drizzle with olive oil and sprinkle with coarsely ground black pepper and finely torn basil leaves. Add a few slices of oven-roasted tomatoes to the ingredients in Slow-cooked Tomato Sauce (see page 192) while the ingredients are simmering for extra depth of flavour. Add thin slices of these tomatoes to Salade Niçoise (see page 118), or Roasted Pepper Salad (see page 160).

Preserved Citrus

Preserved Lemons: makes enough to fill a 2 litre / 3½ pint preserving jar

INGREDIENTS

PRESERVED LEMONS
4 large, thin-skinned,
    unwaxed lemons
about 2 kg/4 lb 8 oz table salt
4 bay leaves

DRIED ORANGE RIND
1 large, unwaxed, sweet orange

1 To make the preserved lemons, rinse the lemons with warm water, then pat dry with kitchen paper. Stand a lemon on its stem end, then cut it into quarters without cutting all the way through. Repeat with the 3 lemons.

2 Spread a 5 mm/¼ inch layer of salt on the bottom of a 2 litre/3½ pint preserving jar with a non-metallic lid. Add one of the lemons, cut-side up, pressing to open out the quarters. Add a bay leaf and enough salt to completely cover. Repeat to make 3 more layers.

3 Using a wooden spoon, press down on the lemons to release their juice. Cover with a layer of salt. Seal the jar and set aside for at least a month, turning the jar upside-down every day.

4 Pull out a lemon quarter when required and rinse well. To use, follow the specific recipe instructions – some recipes use the flesh as well as the rind, while others only use the rind.

5 To make the dried orange rind, use a small, serrated knife to cut the rind off a large orange in a single spiral, starting from the top and working your way to the bottom.

6 Thread a needle with thin thread and stitch it through the orange rind to make a loop to hang the rind from. Hang the rind from a hook in your kitchen until it is dry. Store in an airtight jar and use as required.

Candied Citrus Peel

Makes 60–80 pieces

INGREDIENTS

1 large, thick-skinned, unwaxed orange	1 large, thick-skinned, unwaxed lime	125 g/4½ oz best-quality dark chocolate, chopped (optional)
1 large, thick-skinned, unwaxed lemon	600 g/1 lb 5 oz caster sugar	
	300 ml/10 fl oz water	

1 Cut the orange into quarters lengthways and squeeze the juice into a cup to drink, or use in another recipe. Cut each quarter in half lengthways to make 8 pieces.

2 Cut the fruit and pith away from the rind. If any of the pith remains on the rind, lay the knife almost flat on the white side of the rind and gently 'saw' backwards and forwards to slice it off because it will make the peel taste bitter.

3 Repeat with the lemon and lime, only cutting the lime into quarters. Cut each piece into 3 or 4 thin strips to make 60–80 strips in total. Place the strips in a pan of water and boil for 30 seconds. Drain.

4 Dissolve the sugar in the water in a pan over a medium heat, stirring. Increase the heat and bring to the boil, without stirring. When the syrup becomes clear, turn the heat to its lowest setting.

5 Add the citrus strips, using a wooden spoon to push them in without stirring. Simmer in the syrup for 30 minutes, without stirring. Turn off the heat and set aside for at least 6 hours until completely cool.

6 Line a baking sheet with foil. Skim off the thin crust on top of the syrup without stirring. Remove the rind strips, one by one, from the syrup, shaking off any excess. Place the strips on the foil to cool.

7 If you want to dip candied peel in chocolate, melt the chocolate. Working with one piece of candied peel at a time, dip the peel half-way into the chocolate. Return to the foil and leave to dry. Store in an airtight container when completely dry.

Mediterranean Fish Stock

Makes about 2 litres / 3½ pints

INGREDIENTS

1 kg/2 lb 4 oz fish bones and
trimmings
at least 3 litres/5¼ pints water
pinch of salt
4 large tomatoes

2 large bulbs of fennel
2 large garlic cloves
1 leek
125 ml/4 fl oz dry white wine

1 bouquet garni of 2 sprigs fresh
flat-leaved parsley and
1 sprig fresh thyme, tied in a
7.5 cm/3 inch piece celery

1 Rinse the fish bones and trimmings under cold running water, wiping off any blood. Place them in a large flameproof casserole or stockpot and pour over the water. Add a pinch of salt and heat until almost boiling with bubbles just breaking the surface, but do not let the liquid boil.

2 Using a large spoon, skim the surface. Lower the heat to the lowest setting and simmer the stock, uncovered, for 30 minutes, skimming the surface as necessary to remove scum.

3 Meanwhile, chop the tomatoes, fennel and garlic. Slice the leek, then chop and rinse well in a bowl of cold water.

4 Strain the fish stock from the casserole or stockpot into a large bowl and discard the solids.

5 Return the stock to the washed-out casserole or stockpot and add the vegetables, wine and bouquet garni. Slowly bring to the boil, skimming the surface with a spoon as necessary.

6 Lower the heat, partially cover the casserole, and simmer for a further 30 minutes, or until reduced to about 2 litres/3½ pints. Strain the stock into a large bowl and leave to cool. Refrigerate until required.

COOK'S TIP

This will keep in the refrigerator, covered, for 2 days.

Greek Strained Yogurt

Makes about 500 g / 1 lb 2 oz

INGREDIENTS

1 kg/2 lb 4 oz natural yogurt
½ tsp salt, or to taste

OPTIONAL TOPPINGS
fruity extra-virgin olive oil
orange-blossom or lavender-
    flavoured honey
finely grated lemon rind

coriander seeds, crushed
powdered paprika
very finely chopped fresh mint
    or coriander

1 Place a 125 x 75 cm/50 x 30 inch piece of muslin in a saucepan, cover with water and bring to the boil. Remove the pan from the heat and, using a wooden spoon, lift out the muslin. Wearing rubber gloves, wring the cloth dry.

2 Fold the cloth into a double layer and use it to line a colander or sieve set over a large bowl. Put the yogurt in a bowl and stir in the salt. Spoon the yogurt into the centre of the cloth.

3 Tie the cloth so it is suspended above the bowl. If your sink is deep enough, gather up the corners of the cloth and tie it to the tap. If not, lay a broom handle across 2 chairs and put the bowl between the chairs. Tie the cloth to the broom handle. Remove the colander or sieve and leave the yogurt to drain into the bowl for at least 12 hours.

4 Transfer the thickened drained yogurt to a nylon sieve sitting over a bowl. Cover lightly with cling film

and keep in the refrigerator for another 24 hours until soft and creamy. This yogurt will keep refrigerated for up to 5 days.

5 To serve, taste and add extra salt if needed. Spoon the yogurt into a bowl and sprinkle with the topping of your choice, or a combination of toppings.

Aioli

Makes about 350 ml / 12 fl oz

INGREDIENTS

4 large garlic cloves, or to taste
pinch of sea salt
2 large egg yolks
300 ml/10 fl oz extra-virgin
    olive oil
1–2 tbsp lemon juice, to taste
1 tbsp fresh white breadcrumbs

salt and pepper

CRUDITES (TO SERVE)
a selection of raw vegetables,
    such as sliced red peppers,
    courgette slices, whole spring
    onions and tomato wedges

a selection of blanched and
    cooled vegetables, such as
    baby artichoke hearts,
    cauliflower or broccoli florets
    or French beans

1 Finely chop the garlic on a chopping board. Add the salt to the garlic and use the tip and broad side of a knife to work the garlic and salt into a smooth paste.

2 Transfer the garlic paste to a food processor. Add the egg yolks and process until well blended, stopping to scrape down the side of the bowl with a rubber spatula, if necessary.

3 With the motor running, slowly pour the olive oil in a steady stream through

the feed tube, processing until the mixture forms a thick mayonnaise.

4 Add 1 tablespoon of the lemon juice and the fresh breadcrumbs and quickly process again. Taste and add more lemon juice if necessary. Season to taste with salt and pepper.

5 Place the aioli in a bowl, cover and chill until ready to serve. This will keep for up to 7 days in the refrigerator. To serve as a dip, place the bowl of aioli on a

large platter and surround with a selection of crudités.

COOK'S TIP

The amount of garlic in a traditional Provençal aioli is a matter of personal taste. Local cooks use 2 cloves per person as a rule of thumb, but this version is slightly milder, although still bursting with flavour.

Rouille

Makes about 175 g / 6 oz

INGREDIENTS

60 g/2¼ oz day-old country-style
    white bread
2 large garlic cloves

2 small red chillies
pinch of salt
3 tbsp extra-virgin olive oil

1 tbsp tomato purée
cayenne pepper (optional)
pepper

1 Cut the crusts off the bread. Put the bread in a bowl, pour over water to cover and leave to soak for 30 seconds, or until soft. Squeeze the bread dry, reserving 2 tablespoons of the soaking liquid.

2 Coarsely chop the garlic and chillies. Put them in a mortar with a pinch of salt and pound until they form a paste.

3 Add the paste to the squeezed bread, then continue working in the mortar until the ingredients blend together. Transfer to a bowl and slowly add the olive oil, beating constantly. If the

mixture begins to separate, add a little of the reserved soaking liquid.

4 Add the tomato purée and cayenne pepper to taste. Adjust seasoning. Spread on croûtes and use to float on the surface of seafood soup.

COOK'S TIP

If the sauce appears to be separating after it has stood for a while, stir in 1 tablespoon hot water. If it appears too thin to spread on croûtes, beat in a little extra soaked bread.

VARIATION

For a smoother version, use a small food processor. Put the squeezed bread and chopped garlic and chillies in the food processor and blend. Add the olive oil and tomato purée and blend again until smooth. Adjust the seasoning.

Skordalia

Makes about 350 g / 12 oz

INGREDIENTS

60 g/2¼ oz day-old bread, in one piece	4–6 large garlic cloves, coarsely chopped	2 tbsp white wine vinegar
150 g/5½ oz unblanched almonds	150 ml/5 fl oz extra-virgin olive oil	salt and pepper
		fresh coriander or flat-leaved parsley sprigs, to garnish

1 Cut the crusts off the bread and tear the bread into small pieces. Put in a bowl, pour over enough water to cover and leave to soak for 10–15 minutes. Squeeze the bread dry and set aside.

2 To blanch the almonds, bring a kettle of water to the boil. Put the almonds in a heatproof bowl and pour over enough boiling water to just cover. Leave to stand for 30 seconds, then drain. The skins should slide off easily.

3 Transfer the almonds and garlic to a food processor and process until finely chopped. Add the squeezed bread and process again until well blended.

4 With the motor running, slowly add the olive oil through the feed tube in a steady stream until a thick paste forms. Add the vinegar and process again. Season with salt and pepper to taste.

5 Transfer to a bowl, cover and chill until required. This will keep in the refrigerator for up to 4 days. To serve, garnish with the fresh herb sprigs.

VARIATIONS

Many versions of this rustic sauce exist. For variety, replace the bread with 4 tablespoons well-drained canned cannellini or broad beans. You can replace the white wine vinegar with freshly squeezed lemon juice.

Fresh Tomato Sauce

Makes enough to fill two 500 ml / 18 fl oz jars

INGREDIENTS

1 kg/2 lb 4 oz juicy plum
   tomatoes
4–6 tbsp extra-virgin olive oil

2 tsp sugar
3 tbsp finely torn fresh basil or
   flat-leaved parsley

salt and pepper
pasta shapes, such as fusilli or
   shells, to serve (optional)

1 Bring a kettle of water to
the boil. Cut a small X in
the top of each tomato and
place in 1 or 2 heatproof
bowls. Pour over the boiling
water and leave for 1 minute,
then drain. Work in batches
if necessary.

2 Peel off the skins and
discard, working over a
sieve placed over a bowl to
strain and catch the tomato
juices. Quarter all
the tomatoes and remove
the seeds. Coarsely chop the
flesh into bite-sized dice.

3 Put the tomatoes and
their juice in a bowl. Add
4 tablespoons of the olive oil,
with the sugar and reserved
tomato juice. Season with salt
and pepper to taste. Gently
stir together, adding a little
more olive oil if it is too
thick. Leave the sauce to
stand for at least 30 minutes
before using.

4 When ready to serve, stir
in the fresh herbs. Serve
with cooked pasta shapes.

COOK'S TIPS

*When tomatoes are not
at their peak, Slow-
cooked Tomato Sauce
(see page 192) is a better
option than fresh.*

*If you make the sauce in
advance, cover and chill
for up to 3 days. Twenty
minutes before serving,
remove from the
refrigerator to allow the
sauce to come to room
temperature. Stir in the
herbs just before serving.*

Slow-cooked Tomato Sauce

Makes about 600 ml / 1 pint

INGREDIENTS

2 sprigs fresh parsley	2 tbsp olive oil	2 strips freshly pared lemon rind
2 sprigs fresh thyme	1 large garlic clove, crushed	½ tsp sugar
1 bay leaf	100 g /3½ oz shallots, chopped	salt and pepper
7.5 cm/3 inch piece of celery	300 ml/10 fl oz full-bodied	
1 kg/2 lb 4 oz plum tomatoes	red wine	

1 To make the bouquet garni, use a piece of kitchen string to tie the sprigs of parsley and thyme with the bay leaf in the piece of celery. Set the herbs aside.

2 Coarsely chop the tomatoes – it isn't necessary to remove the skins or seeds because this sauce will be processed in a food mill, which will result in a smooth texture.

3 Heat the olive oil in a deep frying pan with a lid or in a saucepan. Add the garlic and shallots and cook for about 3 minutes, stirring with a wooden spoon, until they have softened.

4 Add the tomatoes, wine, bouquet garni, lemon rind, sugar and salt and pepper to taste. Bring to the boil, stirring. Lower the heat, partially cover and simmer very gently for 1 hour, or until most of the liquid has evaporated. Do not dry out.

5 Remove the pan from the heat and leave the sauce to cool slightly. Remove the bouquet garni and process the sauce,

including the lemon rind, through a food mill, working in batches if necessary.

6 Adjust the seasoning, if necessary, being generous with freshly ground black pepper. If not using the sauce at once, leave to cool, then cover and keep refrigerated for up to 3 days.

Spinach & Herb Orzo

Serves 4

INGREDIENTS

1 tsp salt
250 g/9 oz dried orzo
200 g/7 oz baby spinach leaves
150 g/5½ oz rocket
25 g/1 oz fresh flat-leaved
 parsley leaves

25 g/1 oz fresh coriander leaves
4 spring onions
2 tbsp extra-virgin olive oil
1 tbsp garlic-flavoured olive oil
salt and pepper

TO SERVE
radicchio or other lettuce leaves
60 g/2¼ oz feta cheese, well
 drained and crumbled
 (optional)
lemon slices, to garnish

1 Bring 2 pans of water to the boil, and put 12 ice cubes in a bowl of cold water. Add the salt and orzo to one of the pans, return to the boil and cook for 8–10 minutes, or according to packet instructions, until the pasta is tender, but not too soft.

2 Meanwhile, remove the stems from the spinach if they are tough. Rinse the leaves in several changes of water to remove any dirt and grit. Coarsely chop the rocket, parsley, coriander and the green parts of the spring onions.

3 Put the spinach, rocket, parsley, coriander and spring onions in the other pan of boiling water and blanch for 15 seconds. Drain and transfer to the iced water to preserve the colour.

4 When the spinach, herbs and spring onions are cool, squeeze out all the excess water. Transfer to a small food processor and process. Add the olive oil and

garlic-flavoured oil and process again until the mixture is well blended.

5 Drain the orzo well and stir in the spinach mixture. Toss well and adjust the seasoning.

6 Line a serving platter with radicchio leaves and pile the orzo on top. Sprinkle with feta cheese, if desired, and garnish with lemon slices. Serve hot or leave to cool to room temperature.

Spiced Pilau with Saffron

Serves 4–6

INGREDIENTS

large pinch of good-quality saffron threads	3 tbsp pine kernels	very finely chopped fresh coriander or flat-leaved parsley, to garnish
450 ml/16 fl oz water, boiling	350 g/12 oz long-grain rice (not basmati)	
1 tsp salt	60 g/2¼ oz sultanas or raisins	
25 g/1 oz butter	6 green cardamom pods, shells lightly cracked	
2 tbsp olive oil	6 cloves	
1 large onion, very finely chopped	salt and pepper	

1 Toast the saffron threads in a dry frying pan over a medium heat stirring for 2 minutes, or until they give off their aroma. Immediately tip them on to a plate.

2 Pour the boiling water into a measuring jug, stir in the saffron and 1 teaspoon salt and set aside for at least 30 minutes to infuse.

3 Melt the butter with the oil in a frying pan over a medium–high heat. Add the onion and cook for about 5 minutes, stirring, until it is soft.

4 Lower the heat, stir in the pine kernels and cook for 2 minutes, stirring, until they just start to turn golden. Take care that they do not burn.

5 Stir in the rice, coating all the grains with oil. Stir for 1 minute, then add the sultanas, cardamom pods and cloves. Pour in the saffron-flavoured water and bring to the boil. Lower the heat, cover and simmer for 15 minutes without removing the lid.

6 Remove from the heat and leave to stand for 5 minutes without uncovering. Remove the lid and check that the rice is tender, that all the liquid has been absorbed and that the surface has small indentations all over.

7 Use a fork to fluff up the rice. Adjust the seasoning, stir the herbs through and serve.

Mediterranean Bread

Makes 1 loaf

INGREDIENTS

400 g/14 oz plain flour, plus extra
for sprinkling
1 sachet easy-blend dried yeast
1 tsp salt
1 tbsp coriander seeds, lightly
crushed
2 tsp dried oregano

200 ml/7 fl oz water, heated to
52°C/125°F on an instant-
read thermometer
3 tbsp olive oil, plus extra oil
for greasing

150 g/5½ oz sun-dried tomatoes
in oil, drained, patted dry
and chopped
75 g/2¾ oz feta cheese, drained,
patted dry and cubed
100 g/3½ oz black olives, patted
dry, stoned and sliced

1 Stir the flour, yeast, salt, coriander seeds and oregano together and make a well in the centre. Slowly add most of the water and the olive oil to make a dough. Gradually add the remaining water, if needed, drawing in all the flour.

2 Turn out on to a lightly floured surface and knead for 10 minutes, gradually kneading in the sun-dried tomatoes, cheese and olives. (The cheese will break up as you knead.) Wash the bowl and lightly coat it with oil.

3 Shape the dough into a ball, put it in the bowl and turn the dough over. Cover the bowl tightly and leave the dough until it doubles in volume.

4 Turn the dough out on to a lightly floured surface. Knead lightly, then shape into a ball. Place on a lightly floured baking sheet. Cover and leave to rise until it doubles again.

5 Lightly sprinkle the top with flour. Using a sharp knife, cut 3 shallow slashes in the top. Bake in an oven preheated to 230°C/450°F/Gas Mark 8 for 20 minutes. Lower the heat to 200°C/400°F/Gas Mark 6 and bake for 20 minutes longer, or until the loaf sounds hollow when you tap it on the bottom. Leave to cool completely. This loaf keeps well for up to 3 days in an airtight container.

Sesame Breadsticks

Makes 32 sticks

INGREDIENTS

225 g/8 oz unbleached strong
    white flour
225 g/8 oz strong wholemeal
    flour
1 sachet easy-blend dried yeast

2 tsp salt
½ tsp sugar
450 ml/16 fl oz water, heated to
    52°C/125°F on an instant-
    read thermometer

4 tbsp olive oil, plus extra
    for greasing
1 egg white, lightly beaten
sesame seeds, for sprinkling

1 Stir the flours, yeast, salt and sugar together in a bowl and make a well in the centre. Slowly stir in most of the water and the olive oil to make a dough. Gradually add the remaining water, if necessary, drawing in all the flour to the dough.

2 Turn out on to a lightly floured surface and knead for about 10 minutes until smooth. Wash the bowl and lightly coat with olive oil.

3 Shape the dough into a ball, put it in the bowl and turn over so that it is

coated. Cover tightly with a clean tea towel and leave the dough until it has doubled in volume. Line a baking sheet with baking parchment.

4 Turn out the dough on to a lightly floured surface and knead lightly. Divide into 2 equal pieces. Roll each piece into a 40 cm/ 16 inch rope and cut into 8 equal pieces. Cut each piece in half to make 32 pieces.

5 Cover the dough you are not working with as you roll each piece into a thin

25 cm/10 inch rope, on a very lightly floured surface. Carefully transfer the sticks to the baking sheet.

6 Cover and leave to rise for 10 minutes. Brush with the egg white, then sprinkle thickly and evenly with sesame seeds. Bake in a preheated oven at 230°C/450°F/Gas Mark 8 for 10 minutes.

7 Brush again with egg white, and bake for a further 5 minutes, or until golden brown and crisp. Cool on wire racks.

Olive Rolls

Makes 16 rolls

INGREDIENTS

115 g/4 oz olives in brine or
oil, drained
750 g/1 lb 10 oz unbleached
strong white flour, plus extra
for dusting
1½ tsp salt

1 sachet easy-blend dried yeast
450 ml/16 fl oz water, heated to
52°C/125°F on an instant-
read thermometer
2 tbsp fruity extra-virgin olive oil,
plus extra for brushing

4 tbsp finely chopped fresh
oregano, parsley or thyme
leaves, or 1 tbsp dried
mixed herbs

1 Stone the olives with an olive or cherry pitter and finely chop. Pat off the excess brine or oil with kitchen paper. Set aside.

2 Stir the flour, salt and yeast together in a bowl and make a well in the centre. Slowly stir in most of the water and the olive oil to make a dough. Gradually add the remaining water, if necessary, drawing in all the flour to the dough.

3 Lightly knead in the olives and herbs. Turn out on to a lightly floured surface and knead for 10 minutes. Wash the bowl and lightly coat with oil.

4 Shape the dough into a ball, put it in the bowl and turn over so it is coated. Cover tightly with a tea towel and leave to rest until it doubles in volume. Dust a baking sheet with flour.

5 Turn out the dough on to a lightly floured surface and knead lightly. Roll into 20 cm/8 inch ropes on a lightly floured surface.

6 Cut the dough into 16 even-sized pieces. Shape each one into a ball and place on the prepared baking sheet. Cover and leave to rise for 15 minutes.

7 Lightly brush the top of each roll with olive oil. Bake in a preheated oven at 220°C/425°F/Gas Mark 7 for 25–30 minutes, or until the rolls are golden brown. Cool on a wire rack.

Fougasse

Makes 2 large loaves

INGREDIENTS

750 g/1 lb 10 oz unbleached strong white flour, plus extra for kneading and dusting	1 sachet easy-blend dried yeast 2 tsp salt 1 tsp sugar	450 ml/16 fl oz/2 cups water, heated to 52°C/125°F on an instant-read thermometer olive oil, for greasing

1 Stir the flour, yeast, salt and sugar together in a bowl and make a well in the centre. Slowly stir in most of the water to make a dough. Gradually add the remaining water, drawing in all the flour. If you need extra water, add it gradually, one tablespoon at a time.

2 Turn out on to a lightly floured surface and knead for 10 minutes until smooth. Wash the bowl and lightly coat with olive oil. Shape the dough into a ball, put it in the bowl and turn the dough over. Cover the bowl tightly with a clean tea towel and leave until the dough doubles in volume.

3 Knock back the dough with your fist and turn out on to a lightly floured surface. Knead lightly, then cover with the upturned bowl and leave again for 10 minutes.

4 Put a roasting tin of water in the bottom of the oven while it preheats to 230°C/450°F/Gas Mark 8. Lightly flour a baking sheet.

5 Divide the dough into 2 pieces, and roll each one into a 30 cm/12 inch oval, 1 cm/½ inch thick. Using a sharp knife, cut five 7.5 cm/3 inch slices on an angle in a herringbone pattern on each of the dough ovals. Cut all the way through the dough, using the tip of the knife to open the slits.

6 Spray the loaves with cold water. Bake for 20 minutes, turn upside down and continue baking for 5 minutes until the loaves sound hollow when tapped on the bottom. Cool on wire racks.

Herb Focaccia

Makes 1 loaf

INGREDIENTS

400 g/14 oz unbleached strong white flour, plus extra for dusting	300 ml/10 fl oz water, heated to 52°C/125°F on an instant-read thermometer	4 tbsp finely chopped fresh herbs
1 sachet easy-blend dried yeast		polenta or cornmeal, for sprinkling
1½ tsp salt	3 tbsp good-quality fruity extra-virgin olive oil, plus extra for greasing	coarse sea salt, for sprinkling
½ tsp sugar		

1 Stir the flour, yeast, salt and sugar together in a bowl and make a well in the centre. Slowly stir in most of the water and 2 tablespoons of the olive oil to make a dough. Gradually add the remaining water, if necessary, drawing in all the flour.

2 Turn out on to a lightly floured surface and knead. Transfer to a bowl and lightly knead in the herbs for 10 minutes until soft but not sticky. Wash the bowl and lightly coat with olive oil.

3 Shape the dough into a ball, put it in the bowl and turn the dough over. Cover tightly with a tea towel and leave until the dough doubles in volume. Sprinkle polenta over a baking sheet.

4 Turn the dough out on to a lightly floured surface and knead lightly. Cover with the upturned bowl and leave for 10 minutes.

5 Roll and pat the dough into a 25 cm/10 inch circle, about 1 cm/½ inch thick, and place on the prepared baking sheet. Cover with a tea towel and leave to rise for 15 minutes.

6 Using a lightly oiled finger, poke indentations all over the surface. Drizzle the remaining 1 tablespoon of olive oil over and sprinkle lightly with sea salt. Bake in a preheated oven at 230°C/450°F/Gas Mark 8 for 15 minutes, or until golden and the loaf sounds hollow on the bottom. Cool the loaf on a wire rack.

Sangria

Makes 8–10 glasses

INGREDIENTS

1 large orange
1 lemon
2 peaches

100 g/3½ oz sugar, or to taste
1 litre/1¾ pints full-bodied
    Spanish wine, such as Rioja

10 cm/4 inch piece of cucumber
ice cubes, to serve

1 Cut the orange into thin slices, then cut the slices into wedges. Place in a large ceramic or glass jug. Cut one long strip of rind from the lemon and add to the orange.

2 Slice right around the peaches, cutting down to the stone. Twist the halves in opposite directions, until the two halves come apart. Remove and discard the stones. Slice the peaches and add to the orange.

3 Add the sugar to the fruit and stir. Pour in the wine and stir until the sugar dissolves. Taste and add more

sugar or a squeeze or two of lemon juice to taste. Chill for at least an hour.

4 Meanwhile, dice the piece of cucumber or cut it into stick shapes.

5 When ready to serve, use a long-handled wooden spoon to stir and press the fruit against the side of the jug to extract some of the juice. Put the ice cubes into glasses and pour the chilled sangria over. Add some fruit from the jug to each glass, then add the cucumber. Serve at once.

VARIATIONS

Red wine is traditionally used in this popular drink, but you can use white wine as well. For a party, add a drop of brandy before you chill the sangria. Limes can also be used in this drink.

Desserts

Mediterranean fruits, like the region's vegetables, really benefit in terms of flavour from ripening under the intense sun. They are juicy and succulent, and a platter of simply prepared fruit can make the perfect end to a meal.

For simple recipes that don't adulterate the fruit's natural flavour, try ripe figs with a subtle orange-blossom cream, or Creamy Fruit Parfait, with peaches, apricots and cherries, from the Greek island of Kythera. Or, when strawberries are just past their peak, serve Balsamic Strawberries with Mascarpone – the unlikely combination of ground pepper and balsamic vinegar will highlight any flavour there is left.

However, not all Mediterranean desserts are fruit-based. The Middle Eastern influence on Turkish and Moroccan cooking means very sweet desserts are enjoyed with small cups of strong, dark espresso coffee. Few desserts can be sweeter than Baklava, thin layers of crisp filo pastry filled with spiced and sweetened chopped nuts and soaked in a sugar syrup. If you want something more comforting and homely, there's a Creamy Rice Pudding from Greece flavoured with lemon.

The Italians are known for their excellent ice creams, so try the Lavender Ice Cream or Mint-chocolate Gelato. When you are in a hurry, few desserts can be quicker than Italian Drowned Ice Cream – hot espresso poured over home-made vanilla ice cream.

Balsamic Strawberries with Mascarpone

Serves 4

INGREDIENTS

450 g/1 lb fresh strawberries
2–3 tbsp best-quality
  balsamic vinegar

pepper
fresh mint leaves, torn, plus extra
  to decorate (optional)

115–175 g/4–6 oz mascarpone
cheese

1 Wipe the strawberries with a damp cloth, rather than rinsing them, so they do not become soggy. Using a paring knife, cut off the green stalks at the top and use the tip of the knife to remove the core.

2 Cut each strawberry in half lengthways, or into quarters if large. Transfer the fruit to a bowl.

3 Add the vinegar, allowing ½ tablespoon per person. Add several twists of ground black pepper, then gently stir together. Cover the dish with clingfilm and chill for up to 4 hours.

4 Just before serving, stir in torn mint leaves to taste. Spoon the mascarpone cheese into individual bowls and spoon the berries on top. Decorate with a few mint leaves, if wished. Sprinkle with extra pepper to taste.

VARIATION

Replace the mascarpone cheese with Vanilla Ice Cream (see page 228), or a premium commercial vanilla or strawberry ice cream.

COOK'S TIP

This is most enjoyable when it is made with the best-quality balsamic vinegar, one that has aged slowly and has turned thick and syrupy. Unfortunately, the genuine mixture is always expensive. Less expensive versions are artificially sweetened and coloured with caramel, or taste of harsh vinegar.

Figs with Orange-blossom Cream

Serves 4

INGREDIENTS

8 large fresh figs
4 large fresh fig leaves, if
   available, rinsed and dried

CREME FRAICHE (OPTIONAL)
2 tbsp buttermilk

300 ml/10 fl oz double cream

ORANGE-BLOSSOM CREAM
125 ml/4 fl oz crème fraîche,
   home-made (see below)
   or bought

about 4 tbsp orange-
   blossom water
1 tsp orange-blossom honey
finely grated rind of ½ orange
2 tbsp flaked almonds, to
   decorate (optional)

1 If you are making the
crème fraîche, begin at
least a day ahead. Put the
buttermilk in a preserving jar
or a jar with a screw top. Add
the cream, securely close and
shake to blend. Leave to set at
warm room temperature for
6–8 hours, then refrigerate
for at least 8 hours and up to
4 days. It will develop a
slightly tangy flavour. Lightly
beat before using.

2 To toast the almonds
for the decoration, place
in a dry frying pan over a
medium heat and stir until

lightly browned. Take care
that they do not burn.
Immediately tip the almonds
out of the pan. Set aside.

3 To make the orange-
blossom cream, put the
crème fraîche in a small bowl
and stir in 4 tablespoons of
the orange-blossom water,
with the honey and orange
rind. Taste and add a little
extra orange-blossom water
if necessary.

4 To serve, cut the stems
off the figs, but do not
peel them. Stand the figs

upright with the pointed end
upwards. Cut each into
quarters without cutting all
the way through, so that you
can open them out into
attractive 'flowers'.

5 If you are using fig
leaves, place one in the
centre of each serving plate.
Arrange 2 figs on top of each
leaf, and spoon a small
amount of the orange-
flavoured cream alongside
them. Sprinkle the cream
with the toasted flaked
almonds if desired, just
before serving.

Oranges in Spiced Caramel

Serves 4

INGREDIENTS

4 large, juicy oranges
4–6 tbsp shelled pistachio nuts,
   chopped, to decorate

SPICED CARAMEL
250 g/9 oz caster sugar
5 black peppercorns, lightly
   crushed

4 cloves
1 green cardamom pod,
   lightly crushed
300 ml/10 fl oz water

1 To make the spiced
caramel, put the sugar,
peppercorns, cloves,
cardamom pod and 150 ml/
5 fl oz of the water in a pan
and stir to dissolve the sugar
over a medium heat. When
the sugar has dissolved, turn
up the heat and boil, without
stirring, until the syrup
thickens and turns a deep
caramel colour. Use a wet
pastry brush to brush down
the side of the pan if
necessary.

2 Very carefully, pour in
another 150 ml/5 fl oz
water, standing back because

it will splatter. Remove from
the heat and, using a long-
handled wooden spoon, stir
until all the caramel has
dissolved. Set aside to cool.

3 Pare off the orange rind
and pith, cutting
carefully so the oranges
retain their shape. Leave the
oranges whole, or, working
over a bowl, cut into
segments, cutting the flesh
away from the membranes.

4 Pour over the caramel
syrup with the spices and
stir together. Cover and chill
until ready to serve. Serve in

individual bowls with
chopped pistachio nuts
sprinkled over the tops at the
last minute.

VARIATION

*Turn this Spanish
dessert into a Sicilian-
style one by using the
blood-red oranges that
grow in great profusion
on the island.*

Creamy Fruit Parfait

Serves 4–6

INGREDIENTS

225 g/8 oz fresh, juicy cherries
2 large peaches
2 large apricots

700 ml/1¼ pints Greek Strained
  Yogurt (see page 182), or
  natural thick yogurt
60 g/2¼ oz walnut halves

2 tbsp flower-scented honey,
  or to taste
fresh redcurrants or berries, to
  decorate (optional)

1 To prepare the fruit, use a cherry or olive stoner to remove the cherry stones. Cut each cherry in half. Cut the peaches and apricots in half lengthways and remove the stones, then finely chop the flesh.

2 Place the prepared cherries, peaches and apricots in a bowl and gently stir the fruit together.

3 Spoon one-third of the yogurt into an attractive glass serving bowl. Top with half the fruit mixture.

4 Repeat with another layer of yogurt and fruit; top with the remaining yogurt.

5 Place the walnuts in a small food processor and pulse until chopped but not finely ground. Sprinkle the walnuts over the top layer of the yogurt.

6 Drizzle the honey over the nuts and yogurt. Cover the bowl with clingfilm and chill for at least 1 hour. Decorate with a small bunch of redcurrants, if using, just before serving.

VARIATION

Vary the fruit to whatever is best in the market. Berries, figs, seedless grapes and melons are also delicious in this simple family-style dessert. In winter, replace the fresh fruit salad with a dried fruit compote: cover dried fruit, such as apples, apricots, stoned dates and figs, in orange juice, leave to plump, then proceed with the recipe.

Peaches with Amaretto-Mascarpone

Serves 4–6

INGREDIENTS

8–12 ripe peaches
1 large lime
450 ml/16 fl oz fruity dry
    white wine
1 tbsp black peppercorns,
    lightly crushed

7.5 cm/3 inch cinnamon stick,
    halved lengthways
finely pared rind of
    1 unwaxed lemon
100 g/3½ oz caster sugar
fresh mint sprigs, to decorate

AMARETTO-MASCARPONE
    CREAM
2 tbsp amaretto liqueur, or
    to taste
250 g/9 oz mascarpone cheese

1 Fill a large bowl with iced water. Bring a large pan of water to the boil. Add the peaches and cook for 1 minute. Using a slotted spoon, immediately transfer the peaches to the iced water to stop the cooking process.

2 Squeeze the juice from the lime into a bowl of water. Peel the peaches, then quarter each and remove the stone. Drop the fruit into the lime water as it is prepared. Cover and refrigerate for 24 hours.

3 Meanwhile, make the amaretto-mascarpone cream. Stir the amaretto into the mascarpone, cover and refrigerate.

4 Place the wine, peppercorns, cinnamon, lemon rind and sugar in a saucepan over a medium-high heat, and stir until the sugar dissolves.

5 Boil the syrup for 2 minutes. Reduce to a simmer. Remove the peaches, add them to the

syrup and poach for 2 minutes, or until tender (they should not end up falling apart).

6 Using a slotted spoon, transfer the peaches to a bowl. Bring the syrup to the boil and continue boiling until thickened and reduced to about 125 ml/4 fl oz. Pour the syrup into a heatproof bowl and leave to cool. When cool, pour over the peaches. Cover and chill until required. To serve, decorate with mint sprigs.

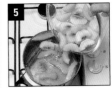

Creamy Rice Pudding with Lemon & Pistachio Nuts

Serves 4

INGREDIENTS

1 tsp cornflour	about 2 tbsp sugar, or 1 tbsp	freshly squeezed lemon juice,
850 ml/1½ pints milk, plus an	honey, to taste	to taste
extra 2 tbsp	finely grated rind of	50 g/1¾ oz shelled pistachio
125 g/4½ oz short-grain rice	1 large lemon	nuts, chopped

1 Place the cornflour in a small bowl and stir in 2 tablespoons milk, stirring until no lumps remain. Rinse a pan with cold water and do not dry it out.

2 Place the remaining milk and the cornflour mixture in the pan over a medium–high heat, stirring occasionally, until it simmers and forms small bubbles all around the edge. Do not boil.

3 Stir in the rice, lower the heat and continue stirring for 20 minutes, or until all but about 2 tablespoons of the excess liquid has evaporated and the rice grains are tender.

4 Remove from the heat and pour into a heatproof bowl. Stir in sugar to taste. Stir the lemon rind into the pudding. If a slightly tarter flavour is required, stir in freshly squeezed lemon juice. Allow to cool completely.

5 Tightly cover the top of the cool rice with a sheet of clingfilm and chill in the refrigerator for at least one hour – the colder the rice is, the better it tastes with fresh fruit.

6 Meanwhile, using a sharp knife, finely chop the pistachio nuts. To serve, spoon the rice pudding into individual bowls and sprinkle with the chopped nuts.

COOK'S TIP

It is important to rinse the saucepan in step 1 to prevent the milk scorching on the sides or base of the pan.

Spanish Flan

Serves 4–6

INGREDIENTS

butter, for greasing	juice of ½ lemon	2 large eggs
175 g/6 oz caster sugar	500 ml/18 fl oz milk	2 large egg yolks
4 tbsp water	1 vanilla pod	

1 Lightly butter the sides of a 1.2 litre/2 pint soufflé dish. To make the caramel, put 75 g/2¾ oz sugar with the water in a pan over a medium-high heat and cook, stirring, until the sugar dissolves. Boil until the syrup turns a deep golden brown.

2 Immediately remove from the heat and add a few drops of lemon juice. Pour into the soufflé dish and swirl around. Set aside.

3 Pour the milk into a pan. Slit the vanilla pod lengthways and add it to the milk. Bring to the boil, remove the pan from the heat and stir in the remaining sugar, stirring until it dissolves. Set aside.

4 Beat the eggs and egg yolks together in a bowl. Pour the milk mixture over them, whisking. Remove the vanilla pod. Strain the egg mixture into a bowl, then transfer to the soufflé dish.

5 Place the dish in a roasting tin filled with enough boiling water to come two-thirds up the side.

6 Bake in a preheated oven at 160°C/325°F/Gas Mark 3 for 75–90 minutes until a knife inserted in the centre comes out clean. Leave to cool completely.

Cover with clingfilm and refrigerate for at least 24 hours.

7 Run a round-bladed knife around the edge of the dish. Place an upturned serving plate with a rim on top, then invert the plate and dish, giving a sharp shake half-way over. Lift off the soufflé dish and serve.

COOK'S TIP

The lemon juice is added to the caramel in step 2 to stop the cooking process, to prevent it from burning.

Orange Crème à Catalanas

Serves 8

INGREDIENTS

1 litre/1¾ pints milk
finely grated rind of 6 large
    oranges

9 large egg yolks
200 g/7 oz caster sugar, plus
    extra for the topping

3 tbsp cornflour

1 Put the milk and orange rind in a saucepan over a medium-high heat. Bring to the boil, then remove from the heat, cover and leave to cool for 2 hours.

2 Return the milk to the heat and simmer for 10 minutes. Put the egg yolks and sugar in a heatproof bowl over a saucepan of boiling water. Whisk until creamy and the sugar dissolved.

3 Add 5 tablespoons of the flavoured milk to the cornflour, stirring until smooth. Stir into the milk. Strain the milk into the eggs, whisking until blended.

4 Rinse out the pan and put a layer of water in the bottom. Put the bowl on top of the pan, making sure the base does not touch the water. Simmer over a medium heat, whisking, until the custard is thick enough to coat the back of a wooden spoon, which can take 20 minutes. Do not boil.

5 Pour into eight 150 ml/ 5 fl oz ramekins and leave to cool. Cover each with a piece of clingfilm and put in the refrigerator to chill for at least 6 hours.

6 When ready to serve, sprinkle the top of each ramekin with a layer of sugar.

Use a kitchen blowtorch to melt and caramelize the sugar. Allow to stand for a few minutes until the caramel hardens, then serve at once. Do not return to the refrigerator or the topping will become soft.

COOK'S TIP

A kitchen blowtorch is the best way to melt the sugar quickly and guarantee a crisp topping. These are sold at good kitchen-supply stores. Alternatively, you can melt the sugar under a preheated hot grill.

Italian Drowned Ice Cream

Serves 4–6

INGREDIENTS

VANILLA ICE CREAM
1 vanilla pod
6 large egg yolks
150 g/5½ oz caster sugar, or

vanilla-flavoured sugar
  (see page 254)
500 ml/18 fl oz milk
250 ml/9 fl oz double cream

about 450 ml/16 fl oz freshly
  made espresso coffee
chocolate-covered coffee beans,
  to decorate

1 To make the ice cream, slit the vanilla pod lengthways and scrape out the tiny brown seeds. Set aside.

2 Put the egg yolks and sugar in a heatproof bowl that will sit over a saucepan with plenty of room underneath. Beat the eggs and sugar together until thick and creamy.

3 Put the milk, cream and vanilla pod in a pan over a low heat and bring to a simmer. Pour the milk over the egg mixture, whisking. Place 2.5 cm/1 inch water in

the bottom of a pan. Place the bowl on top, ensuring the base does not touch the water. Turn the heat to medium-high.

4 Cook the mixture, stirring constantly, until it is thick enough to coat the back of a spoon. Remove from the heat, transfer to a bowl and leave to cool.

5 Churn the mixture in an ice-cream maker, following the manufacturer's instructions. Alternatively, place it in a freezerproof container and freeze for 1 hour. Turn out into a bowl

and whisk to break up the ice crystals, then return to the freezer. Repeat 4 times at 30-minute intervals.

6 Transfer the ice cream to a freezerproof bowl, smooth the top and cover with clingfilm or foil. Freeze for up to 3 months.

7 Soften in the refrigerator for 20 minutes before serving. Place scoops of ice cream in individual bowls. Pour over the hot coffee and sprinkle with chocolate-covered coffee beans.

Mint-chocolate Gelato

Serves 4–6

INGREDIENTS

6 large eggs
150 g/5½ oz caster sugar
300 ml/10 fl oz milk
150 ml/5 fl oz double cream

large handful fresh mint leaves,
rinsed and dried

2 drops green food colouring
(optional)
60 g/2¼ oz dark chocolate,
finely chopped

1 Put the eggs and sugar in a large mixing bowl. Using an electric mixer, beat the eggs and sugar together until thick and creamy.

2 Put the milk and cream in a saucepan and bring to a simmer, where small bubbles appear all around the edge, stirring. Pour on to the eggs and sugar, whisking constantly. Rinse the pan. Turn the heat to medium-high.

3 Transfer the mixture to the pan and cook gently, stirring constantly, until it is thick enough to coat the back of a spoon and leave a mark when you pull your finger across it.

4 Tear the mint leaves and stir them into the custard. Remove the custard from the heat. Leave to cool, then cover and infuse for at least 2 hours, chilling for the last 30 minutes.

5 Strain the mixture through a small nylon sieve, to remove the pieces of mint. Stir in the food colouring, if using. Churn in an ice-cream maker for 20 minutes, adding the chocolate pieces when the mixture becomes thick and

almost frozen. If you don't have an ice-cream maker, freeze and whisk as in Step 5 of Vanilla Ice Cream (see page 228).

6 Transfer to a freezerproof bowl, smooth the top and cover with clingfilm or foil. Freeze for up to 3 months. Soften in the refrigerator for 20 minutes before serving.

Lavender Ice Cream

Serves 6–8

INGREDIENTS

flowers from 10–12 large sprigs fresh lavender, plus extra to decorate	6 large egg yolks 150 g/5½ oz caster sugar, or Lavender Sugar (see Cook's Tip)	500 ml/18 fl oz milk 250 ml/9 fl oz double cream 1 tsp vanilla essence

1 Strip the small flowers from the stems, without any brown or green bits. Place them in a small sieve and rinse, then pat dry with kitchen paper. Set aside.

2 Put the egg yolks and sugar in a heatproof bowl that will sit over a saucepan with plenty of room underneath. Using an electric mixer, beat the eggs and sugar together until they are thick.

3 Put the milk, cream and vanilla essence in a saucepan over a low heat and bring to a simmer, stirring. Pour the hot milk over the egg mixture, whisking constantly.

Rinse the pan and place 2.5 cm/1 inch water in the bottom. Place the bowl on top, making sure the base of the bowl does not touch the water. Turn the heat to medium-high.

4 Cook the mixture, stirring, until it is thick enough to coat the back of a spoon.

5 Remove the custard from the heat and stir in the flowers. Cool, then cover and set aside to infuse for 2 hours, chilling for the last 30 minutes. Strain the mixture through a nylon sieve to remove all the lavender flowers.

6 Churn in an ice-cream maker, following the manufacturer's instructions. Alternatively, freeze and whisk as in Step 5 of Vanilla Ice Cream (see page 228).

7 Transfer to a freezerproof bowl, smooth the top and cover with clingfilm or foil. Freeze for up to 3 months. Soften in the refrigerator for 20 minutes before serving. Decorate with fresh lavender flowers.

COOK'S TIP

To make lavender sugar, put 500 g/1lb 2 oz sugar in a food processor, add 125 g/4½ oz lavender flowers, and blend. Leave in a sealed container for 10 days. Sift out the flower bits and store the sugar in a sealed jar.

Orange & Bitters Sorbet

Serves 4–6

INGREDIENTS

3–4 large oranges
225 g/8 oz caster sugar
600 ml/1 pint water

3 tbsp red Italian bitters, such as Campari
2 large egg whites

fresh mint leaves and Candied Citrus Peel (see page 178), to decorate (optional)

1 Working over a bowl to catch any juice, pare the rind from 3 of the oranges, without removing the bitter white pith. If some of the pith does come off with the rind, use the knife to scrape it off.

2 In a saucepan, dissolve the sugar in the water over a low heat, stirring. Increase the heat and boil for 2 minutes without stirring. Using a wet pastry brush, brush down the side of the pan, if necessary.

3 Remove the pan from the heat and pour into a heatproof non-metallic bowl.

Add the orange rind and leave to infuse while the mixture cools to room temperature.

4 Roll the pared oranges back and forth on the work surface, pressing down firmly. Cut them in half and squeeze 125 ml/4 fl oz juice. If you need more juice, squeeze the extra orange.

5 When the syrup is cool, stir in the orange juice and bitters. Strain into a container, cover and chill for at least 30 minutes.

6 Put the mixture in an ice-cream maker and churn for 15 minutes. Alternatively,

follow the instructions on page 228 (step 5). Whisk the egg whites in a clean bowl until stiff.

7 Add the egg whites to the ice-cream mixture and continue churning for 5 minutes, or according to the manufacturer's instructions. Transfer to a shallow, freezerproof container, cover and freeze for up to 2 months.

8 About 15 minutes before serving, soften in the refrigerator. Scoop into bowls and serve decorated with mint leaves and the Candied Citrus Peel, if wished.

Lemon Granita

Serves 4–6

INGREDIENTS

4 large, unwaxed lemons	700 ml/1¼ pints water	fresh mint sprigs (optional),
100 g/3½ oz caster sugar	scooped-out lemons (optional)	to decorate

1 Pare 6 strips of rind from one lemon, then finely grate the rind from the remaining lemons, being very careful not to remove any bitter white pith.

2 Roll the lemons back and forth on the work surface, pressing down firmly. Cut each in half and squeeze 125 ml/4 fl oz juice. Add the grated rind to the juice. Set the mixture aside.

3 Put the pared strips of lemon rind, sugar and water in a saucepan and stir over a low heat to dissolve the sugar. Increase the heat and boil for 4 minutes, without stirring. Use a wet pastry brush to brush down any spatters on the side of the pan. Remove from the heat, pour into a non-metallic bowl and leave to cool.

4 Remove the strips of rind from the syrup. Stir in the grated rind and juice. Transfer to a shallow metal container, cover and freeze for up to 3 months.

5 Chill serving bowls 30 minutes before serving. To serve, invert the container on to a chopping board. Rinse a cloth in very hot water, wring it out, then rub on the bottom of the container for 15 seconds. Give the container a shake and the mixture should fall out. If not, repeat.

6 Use a knife to break up the granita and transfer to a food processor. Quickly process until it becomes granular. Serve at once in the chilled bowls (or in scooped-out lemons). Decorate with mint sprigs, if wished.

VARIATION

Lemon-scented herbs add a unique flavour. Add 4 small sprigs lemon balm or 2 sprigs lemon thyme to the syrup in Step 3. Remove and discard with the pared rind in Step 4.

Espresso Granita

Serves 4–6

INGREDIENTS

200 g/7 oz caster sugar
600 ml/1 pint water

½ tsp vanilla essence
600 ml/1 pint very strong
  espresso coffee, chilled

fresh mint, to garnish

1 Put the sugar in a saucepan with the water and stir over a low heat to dissolve the sugar. Increase the heat and boil for 4 minutes, without stirring. Use a wet pastry brush to brush down any spatters on the side of the pan.

2 Remove the pan from the heat and pour the syrup into a heatproof non-metallic bowl. Sit the bowl in the kitchen sink filled with iced water to speed up the cooling process. Stir in the vanilla essence and coffee. Leave until completely cool.

3 Transfer to a shallow metal container, cover and freeze for up to 3 months.

4 Thirty minutes before serving the granita, place serving bowls in the refrigerator to chill.

5 To serve, invert the container on to a chopping board. Rinse a cloth in very hot water, wring it out, then rub on the bottom of the container for 15 seconds. Give the container a sharp shake and the mixture should fall out. If not, repeat.

6 Use a knife to break up the granita and transfer to a food processor. Quickly process until it becomes grainy and crunchy. Serve at once in the chilled bowls, decorated with mint.

COOK'S TIP

A very dark, full-flavoured espresso is the only choice for this Italian speciality. Otherwise the flavour will be marred by the freezing.

Italian Ricotta-lemon Cheesecake

Serves 6–8

INGREDIENTS

50 g/1¾ oz sultanas
3 tbsp marsala or grappa
butter, for greasing
semolina, for dusting
350 g/12 oz ricotta cheese,
    drained
3 large egg yolks, beaten
100 g/3½ oz caster sugar

2 tbsp semolina
3 tbsp lemon juice
25 g/1 oz candied orange peel,
    home-made (see page 178) or
    shop-bought, finely chopped
finely grated rind of 2 large
    lemons

TO DECORATE
icing sugar
mint sprigs
fresh redcurrants or other
    berries (optional)

1 Soak the sultanas in the marsala or grappa in a small bowl for about 30 minutes, or until the spirit has been absorbed and the fruit is swollen.

2 Meanwhile, cut out a circle of baking parchment to fit the base of a 20 cm/ 8 inch round cake tin with a removable base that is about 5 cm/2 inches deep. Grease the sides and base of the tin and line the base. Lightly dust with semolina and tip out the excess.

3 Using a wooden spoon, press the ricotta cheese though a nylon sieve into a bowl. Beat in the egg yolks, sugar, semolina and lemon juice, beating until blended.

4 Fold in the sultanas, orange peel and lemon rind. Pour into the prepared tin and smooth the surface.

5 Bake the cheesecake in the centre of a preheated oven at 180°C/350°F/Gas Mark 4 for 30–40 minutes until firm when you press

the top, and slightly coming away from the sides of the tin.

6 Turn off the oven and open the door. Leave the cheesecake to cool in the oven for 2–3 hours. To serve, remove from the pan and transfer to a plate. Sift over a layer of icing sugar from at least 30 cm/12 inches above the cheesecake to lightly dust the top and sides. Decorate with mint and redcurrants, if wished.

Tarte au Citron

Serves 6–8

INGREDIENTS

grated rind of 2–3 large lemons
150 ml/5 fl oz lemon juice
100 g/3½ oz caster sugar
125 ml/4 fl oz double cream or
    crème fraîche

3 large eggs
3 large egg yolks
icing sugar, for dusting

PASTRY
175 g/6 oz plain flour

½ tsp salt
115 g/4 oz cold unsalted
    butter, diced
1 egg yolk, beaten with 2 tbsp
    ice-cold water

1 To make the pastry, sift the flour and salt into a bowl. Using your fingertips, rub the butter into the flour until the mixture resembles fine crumbs. Add the egg yolk and water and stir to make a dough.

2 Gather the dough into a ball, wrap in clingfilm and refrigerate for at least 1 hour. Roll out on a lightly floured work surface and use to line a 23–25 cm/9–10 inch fluted tart tin with a removable base. Prick the base all over with a fork and line with a sheet of baking parchment and baking beans.

3 Bake in a preheated oven at 200°C/400°F/Gas Mark 6 for 15 minutes until the pastry looks set. Remove the paper and beans. Reduce the oven temperature to 190°C/375°F/Gas Mark 5.

4 Beat the lemon rind, lemon juice and sugar together until blended. Slowly beat in the cream, then beat in the eggs and yolks, one by one.

5 Set the pastry case on a baking sheet and pour in the filling. Transfer to the preheated oven and bake the dessert for 20 minutes until the filling is set.

6 Leave to cool completely on a wire rack. Dust the tart with icing sugar. Serve with Candied Citrus Peel (see page 178).

Chocolate Pine Kernel Tartlets

Makes 8 tartlets

INGREDIENTS

60 g/2¼ oz plain chocolate with
    at least 70% cocoa solids
60 g/2¼ oz unsalted butter
175 g/6 oz caster sugar
75 g/2¼ oz light brown sugar
6 tbsp milk
3½ tbsp golden syrup

finely grated rind of 2 large
    oranges and 2 tbsp freshly
    squeezed juice
1 tsp vanilla essence
3 large eggs, lightly beaten
100 g/3½ oz pine kernels

PASTRY
250 g/9 oz plain flour
pinch of salt
100 g/3½ oz butter
115 g/4 oz icing sugar
1 large egg and 2 large egg yolks

1 To make the pastry, sift the flour and a pinch of salt into a bowl. Make a well in the centre and add the butter, icing sugar, whole egg and egg yolks. Using your fingertips, mix the ingredients in the well into a paste.

2 Gradually incorporate the surrounding flour to make a soft dough. Quickly and lightly knead the dough, then shape into a ball, wrap in clingfilm and chill for at least 1 hour.

3 Roll the pastry into eight 15 cm/6 inch circles. Use to line eight 10 cm/4 inch tartlet tins with removable bases. Line each tartlet with baking parchment, cut to fit, and sprinkle with baking beans. Chill for 10 minutes.

4 Bake in a preheated oven at 200°C/400°F/Gas Mark 6 for 5 minutes. Remove the paper and beans and bake for a further 8 minutes. Leave to cool on a wire rack. Reduce the oven

temperature to 180°C/350°F/Gas Mark 4.

5 Meanwhile, break the chocolate into a saucepan over medium heat. Add the butter and stir until blended.

6 Stir in the remaining ingredients. Spoon the filling into the tartlet cases on a baking sheet. Bake for 25–30 minutes, or until the tops puff up and crack and feel set. Cover with baking parchment for the final 5 minutes if the pastry is browning too much. Transfer to a wire rack and leave to cool for at least 15 minutes before unmoulding. Serve the tartlets warm or at room temperature (not chilled).

Baklava

Makes 25 pieces

INGREDIENTS

300 g/10 oz walnut halves
200 g/7 oz shelled pistachio nuts
100 g/3½ oz blanched almonds
4 tbsp pine kernels, finely
    chopped
finely grated rind of 2 large
    oranges
6 tbsp sesame seeds
1 tbsp sugar

½ tsp ground cinnamon
½ tsp ground mixed spice
about 300 g/10½ oz butter,
    melted
23 sheets filo pastry, each
    25 cm/10 inches square,
    defrosted if frozen

SYRUP
600 g/1 lb 5 oz caster sugar
500 ml/18 fl oz water
5 tbsp honey
3 cloves
2 large strips lemon rind

1 To make the filling, put the walnuts, pistachio nuts, almonds and pine kernels in a food processor and pulse until finely chopped but not ground. Transfer to a bowl and stir in the orange rind, sesame seeds, sugar, cinnamon and mixed spice.

2 Butter a 25 cm/10 inch square ovenproof dish that is 5 cm/2 inches deep. Cut the stacked sheets of filo pastry to size, using a ruler.

Keep them covered with a damp tea towel.

3 Place a sheet of filo on the bottom of the dish and brush with melted butter. Top with 7 more sheets, brushing with butter between each layer.

4 Sprinkle with 125 g/ 4½ oz of the filling. Top with 3 more sheets of filo, brushing each one with butter. Continue layering until all the filo and filling

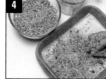

are used, ending with a top layer of 3 sheets of filo. Brush with butter.

5 Using a very sharp knife and a ruler, cut into twenty-five 5 cm/2 inch squares. Brush again with butter. Bake in a preheated oven at 160°C/325°F/Gas Mark 3 for 1 hour.

6 Meanwhile, put all the syrup ingredients in a saucepan, stirring to dissolve the sugar. Bring to the boil, then simmer for 15 minutes, without stirring, until a thin syrup forms. Leave to cool.

7 Remove the baklava from the oven and pour the syrup over the top. Leave to set in the dish.

Cannoli

Makes about 20 rolls

INGREDIENTS

3 tbsp lemon juice
3 tbsp water
1 large egg
250 g/9 oz plain flour
1 tbsp caster sugar
1 tsp ground mixed spice
pinch of salt
25 g/1 oz butter, softened

sunflower oil, for deep-frying
1 small egg white, lightly beaten
icing sugar

FILLING
750 g/1 lb 10 oz ricotta
   cheese, drained
4 tbsp icing sugar
1 tsp vanilla essence

finely grated rind of 1 large
   orange
4 tbsp very finely chopped
   glacé fruit
50 g/1¾ oz plain chocolate,
   grated
pinch of ground cinnamon
2 tbsp marsala or orange juice

1 Combine the lemon juice, water and egg. Put the flour, sugar, spice and salt in a food processor and quickly process. Add the butter, then, with the motor running, pour the egg mixture through the feed tube. Process until the mixture just forms a dough.

2 Turn the dough out on to a lightly floured surface and knead lightly. Wrap and chill for at least 1 hour.

3 Meanwhile, make the filling. Beat the ricotta cheese in a bowl until smooth. Sift in the icing sugar, then beat in the remaining ingredients. Cover and chill until required.

4 Roll out the dough on a floured surface until 2 mm/¹⁄₁₆ inch thick. Using a ruler, cut out 9 x 7.5 cm/ 3½ x 3 inch pieces, re-rolling and cutting the trimmings, to make about 20 pieces.

5 Heat 5 cm/2 inches oil in a pan to 190°C/375°F. Roll a piece of pastry around a greased cannoli mould, to just overlap the edge. Seal with egg white, pressing firmly. Repeat with all the moulds you have. Fry 2 or 3 moulds until golden.

6 Remove with a slotted spoon and drain on kitchen paper. Leave until cool, then carefully slide off the moulds. Repeat with the remaining pastry.

7 Store unfilled in an airtight container for up to 2 days. Pipe in the filling no more than 30 minutes before serving to prevent the pastry becoming soggy. Sift icing sugar over and serve.

Lavender Hearts

Makes about 48 biscuits

INGREDIENTS

225 g/8 oz plain flour, plus extra
    for dusting
75 g/2¾ oz chilled butter, diced
75 g/2¾ oz Lavender Sugar,
    (see page 232), or ordinary
    caster sugar

1 large egg
1 tbsp dried lavender flowers,
    very finely chopped

TO DECORATE
about 4 tbsp icing sugar
about 1 tsp water
about 2 tbsp fresh lavender
    flowers

1 Line 2 baking sheets with baking parchment. Put the flour in a bowl, add the butter and lightly rub in with your fingertips until the mixture resembles fine crumbs. Stir in the lavender sugar.

2 Lightly beat the egg, then add to the flour and butter mixture with the dried lavender flowers. Stir the mixture to form a stiff paste.

3 Turn out the dough on to a lightly floured work surface and roll out until about 5 mm/¼ inch thick.

4 Using a 5 cm/2 inch heart-shaped biscuit cutter, press out 48 biscuits, occasionally dipping the cutter into extra flour, and re-rolling the trimmings as necessary. Transfer the pastry hearts to the baking sheets.

5 Prick the surface of each heart with a fork. Bake in a preheated oven at 180°C/350°F/Gas Mark 4 for 10 minutes, or until lightly browned. Transfer to a wire rack set over a sheet of baking parchment to cool.

6 Sift the icing sugar into a bowl. Add 1 teaspoon cold water and stir until a thin, smooth icing forms, adding a little extra water if necessary.

7 Drizzle the icing from the tip of the spoon over the cooled biscuits in a random pattern. Immediately sprinkle with the fresh lavender flowers while the icing is still soft so that they stick in place. Leave for at least 15 minutes until the icing has set. Store the biscuits for up to 4 days in an airtight container.

Almond Biscuits

Makes about 32 biscuits

INGREDIENTS

150 g/5½ oz unblanched almonds

225 g/8 oz butter, softened

6 tbsp icing sugar, plus extra for sifting

275 g/9½ oz plain flour

2 tsp vanilla essence

½ tsp almond essence

1 Line 2 baking sheets with baking parchment. Using a cook's knife, finely chop the almonds, or process them in a small food processor, taking care not to let them turn into a paste. Set aside.

2 Put the butter in a bowl and beat with an electric mixer until smooth. Sift in the icing sugar and continue beating until the mixture is creamed and smooth.

3 Sift in the flour from above the bowl and gently beat it in until blended. Add the vanilla and almond essences and beat again to form a soft dough. Stir in the chopped almonds.

4 Using a teaspoon, shape the dough into 32 round balls about the size of walnuts. Place on the prepared baking sheets, spacing them apart. Bake in a preheated oven at 180°C/350°F/Gas Mark 4 for 20–25 minutes until the biscuits are set and just starting to turn brown.

5 Leave the biscuits to stand on the baking sheets for 2 minutes to firm up. Sift a thick layer of icing sugar over them. Transfer to a wire rack and leave to cool completely.

6 Lightly dust with more icing sugar, just before serving. Store the biscuits in an airtight container.

VARIATION

Although not a true Mediterranean ingredient, pecan nuts can be used instead of the almonds. Alternatively, add 2 teaspoons finely grated orange rind to the dough in Step 3.

Vanilla Tea Cake with Glacé Fruit

Makes 12–15 slices

INGREDIENTS

225 g/8 oz quality glacé fruit, such as cherries and orange, lemon and lime peels, or Candied Citrus Peel (see page 178)
85 g/3 oz ground almonds
finely grated rind of ½ lemon

85 g/3 oz plain flour
85 g/3 oz self-raising flour
175 g/6 oz butter, softened, plus extra for greasing
175 g/6 oz vanilla-flavoured sugar (see Cook's Tip)

½ tsp vanilla essence
3 large eggs, lightly beaten
pinch of salt
glacé fruit, to decorate

---

1 Grease a 22 x 12 x 5 cm/ 8½ x 4½ x 2 inch loaf tin and line the base with a piece of baking parchment.

2 Chop the fruit into small pieces, reserving a few larger slices for the top. Combine with the ground almonds, lemon rind and 2 tablespoons of the measured plain flour. Set aside.

3 Beat the butter and sugar together until creamy.

Beat in the vanilla essence and eggs, a little at a time.

4 Sift both flours and the salt into the creamed mixture, then fold in. Fold in the fruit and ground almonds.

5 Spoon into the tin and smooth the surface. Arrange the reserved fruit slices on the top. Loosely cover the tin with foil, making sure it does not touch the cake. Bake in a

preheated oven at 180°C/350°F/Gas Mark 4 for about 1½ hours until risen and a skewer inserted into the centre comes out clean.

6 Cool in the tin on a wire rack for 5 minutes. Turn out, remove lining and cool completely. Wrap in foil and store in an airtight container for up to 4 days. Serve decorated with glacé fruit.

COOK'S TIP

Make your own vanilla-flavoured sugar by storing a sliced vanilla pod in a closed jar of caster sugar.

Index